I GOT HERE.
YOU CAN TOO!

By Bruce A. Berman

I Got Here. You Can Too!

T E S T I M O N I A L S

"*'The Berman Differential' changed my life. I was a business student fresh out of college and I wanted to start an online retail business and had no idea where or how to start a business.* After reading 'The Berman Differential,' I learned everything I needed to know. I formed my company, raised money, formed strategic alliances, test marketed my product, and got my business started. I found 'The Berman Differential' program simple to use and more applicable to starting a business than anything I had learned in college."

Chris Boden
Founder, Guys Unlimited

"I began to use Bruce Berman's business strategies when I was 27 years old and co-founded a telecommunications company. *Those strategies helped my company raise $5,000,000 and grow from a startup company with no revenues to a now profitable public company. Last year our revenues topped $17,000,000. I highly recommend 'The Berman Differential' program* for anyone who wants to start or grow a business."

Eric Clemons
President, GTC Telecom

"During my first five years as a chiropractor I was working over fifty hours a week for someone else. I was not only making my employer a lot of money, I had growth limitations set upon myself by my working environment. I decided it was time to start my own medical practice. I needed a business plan, basic business advice, and to raise several hundred thousand dollars. *After being introduced to 'The Berman Differential' method of doing business, in two months I completed and implemented my business plan, raised $430,000, and opened my rehabilitation clinic*. I am proud to say I now have a thriving chiropractic practice and I am my own boss. *I highly urge anyone wanting to be their own boss or grow their existing business to try 'The Berman Differential.'*"

Joseph A. Murphy, D.C.
Newport Mesa Rehabilitation Clinic
Clinical Director

iii.

A B O U T   T H E   A U T H O R

Bruce Berman has a proven track record demonstrating his ability to create, build, and finance moneymaking opportunities from the idea stage to multi-million-dollar companies for both himself and others.

He describes his formal schooling as "barely a high school graduate" (bottom third of his class). When asked how he was able to make millions of dollars without a college education, Bruce Berman responded, "I earned my Master's in Making Millions one business deal at a time."

Bruce Berman was nominated by Sprint for the prestigious Ernst & Young Entrepreneur of the Year award.

In 1999 Bruce Berman thought of an idea for a new business and within 4 $1/2$ months he had raised $4,000,000, built the management team, launched the business, and took the company public. On the second day of trading (only 4 $1/2$ months from the original idea), Mr. Berman's stock was worth $58,000,000.

Bruce Berman had the foresight to pioneer the wind energy industry in the 1980s, and in less than three years his companies employed over 200 people and were responsible for building over $200,000,000 of wind energy facilities.

He created "The Berman Differential" program to assist a wide spectrum of people beginning with the person who has no idea of how to make money or start a business, to the person who has the desire in business to create, start, operate, grow, fund, buy, sell, merge, or take a company public.

I Got Here. You Can Too!

Published by:

Berman Investment Group, LLC.

877-237-6264

Newport Beach, CA 92660

The book you are about to read is based on the business experience of its author, Bruce A. Berman, as well as information he has read or come in contact with. Mr. Berman does not hold any legal, accounting, or college degrees nor does he or has he ever held a securities license.

This book is sold with the understanding that neither the publisher nor the author are engaged in offering legal, securities, or other professional advice. Any actions with regard to the information contained in this book should be undertaken only with the advice and counsel of a trained legal professional.

Library of Congress Cataloging in Process.
ISBN 0-9744998-0-3
Printed in the United States of America.
Proof Edited by Amy Covington
Cover Design by Drive-ID
Cover Photo by Erik Buker
Layout Consulting by JD Designs

D E D I C A T I O N

This book would not have been possible without the lessons I have learned from my mentors, especially "The Professor." May he rest in peace. It's also dedicated to:

All the entrepreneurs who are going to use the tools laid out in this book and my program, "The Berman Differential," to journey on the road of their financial destiny.

Every investor, employee, employer, lawyer, accountant, business owner, business partner, banker, and friend who have crossed my path and participated in my lifetime of lessons in this "book of secrets."

Special Thanks

To my little sister, Linda, for her help in editing this book.

My assistant and nephew, Michael, who is taking his Master's Course in Becoming a Millionaire while working on this book with me, and for the tireless hours he spent with me smoking cigars as we worked late into the night to get this done.

My friend and mentor, Cary, who told me, "When I finish the book, I am a success no matter how many copies are sold."

My children Joshua, Randi, and Grayson for allowing their dad to share his time with others and,

To my mom and dad for never giving up on me.

TABLE OF CONTENTS

WHO ARE AMERICA'S
MILLIONAIRES?

America's millionaires are people with the desire to be rich, who acquired the knowledge and tools necessary to succeed. Desire, knowledge and the necessary tools are the three key ingredients to success. By obtaining a copy of this book, you have expressed the desire to make and keep more money.

Your interest in making money is shared by the wealthiest and most famous people in the world, as well as up-and-coming business owners who make millions running their own companies. The desire to make money is one of the most important ingredients in making millions, but make no mistake about it, the most cost-effective method of creating wealth is accomplished by building a business that continuously pays you, long after you stop actively participating in it. The people who achieve this type of wealth have all learned the same lessons: If you want to reach millionaire, or higher, status and enjoy the freedom that comes with it, you must be your own boss.

When you open the business section of the newspaper you will see article after article about successful people in business. You will read stories like that of Carl Karcher, who started his business with a push cart and parlayed the revenues into the Carl's Junior franchise. So don't laugh when I explain how you can turn $1,000 into $1,000,000 with something as simple as a bubble gum vending machine route, or how you can turn a start-up business into a $100,000,000 public company. What you won't find in the newspaper is a story about John Smith, who took a real estate get-rich-quick program and now is living the life of luxury. Now you may find an ad for one of the several "me too, get rich" real estate programs but not a news worthy story. Why is it not news worthy? Because it rarely happens.

I recognized that money bought what I wanted at an early age. I also knew working for someone else wasn't going to be the answer to getting ahead, so I started my first business at a young age. Since then I have made millions of dollars owning and operating my own businesses.

You are in business whether you realize it or not. Life is a business. When you buy your first car it's you against the automobile salesperson. Negotiating skills can be the difference of thousands of dollars in your pocket when you buy a car. What about renting or buying a home? Marketing, finance, contracts, legal and tax issues can severely impact your pocket book. The chapters in this book will not only help you in the business world but they will assist you in the "business of life."

This book is meant to supplement your desire to be successful with the knowledge you will need. With desire being the first ingredient and knowledge being the second, when you finish this book you will be ready for the third most crucial piece of the financial pie: tools. In my Berman Differential™ program I continue passing on my knowledge and tools to you, so make sure you get a copy of the complete Berman Differential™ software program and use it!

The Berman Differential; A Different Kind Of Education

Do you need a college education to make millions?

No. With a 2.2 high school grade point average and a poor attendance record, I only graduated from high school because of a loophole in a California law. In fact, I graduated in the bottom third of my class. College? Not for this guy. However, I did take a stab or two at junior college, but never completed one course. Don't get me wrong, I want my children to go to college. *It's just my experience, as well as others' experiences, that have demonstrated to me over and over that you can make*

millions of dollars with, or without, a formal college education.

Some people go to school and study music, business, psychology, and math, etc. I studied the art of making the business deal. The only difference between my schooling and those who attended brick and mortar universities is that the people I learned from didn't teach in colleges. My assignments were real, and instead of receiving letter grades I received numbers (the numbers have dollar signs in front of them and they make up your net worth, not your report card).

Don't get me wrong, this is not an anti-college book. It is a pro real-life education book. Real-life education is a different kind of learning experience. It is one that is based on actual business deals, some that were successful and others that didn't go as planned. A regular college professor doesn't meet the prerequisite to teach the real-life education course, as this is a course in making (and keeping) millions of dollars.

Starting when I was in grade school, my business experience has developed uniquely over my lifetime. **In March 2000, I was nominated by Sprint for the Ernst & Young Entrepreneur of the Year award. I have been featured on the cover of several business magazines, as well as being featured on the front page of the Los Angeles Times Business Section.**

I have a proven track record demonstrating my ability to create, build, and finance money-making opportunities from the idea stage, to profitable ventures for my clients and myself. I have owned or been the beneficial owner of numerous companies, including two NASD licensed stock brokerage firms. I have been the majority shareholder and founder of a publicly traded holding company, international manufacturing, national energy-producing firms in both renewable energy and oil and gas fields, finance and equipment leasing firms, financial services websites, consumer retail stores, and more. My companies were either bought public, sold, merged, acquired, or reorganized. ***I have made millions of dollars in my own career and assisted many of my clients as they acquired millions. Companies I have assisted have not only grown into companies with revenues over $75,000,000 annually, but have become public companies with substantial market valuations.***

In fact, in the late 1970s, I provided financing for the mobile communications equipment of a company, then known as National Subscription Television. ***Today that company is known as HBO.***

For years the rich have passed business secrets down from generation to generation. I have accumulated business secrets and amassed strategies from mentors as well as being involved repeatedly in million-dollar business situations. The average person has not come in contact with the secrets I am going to reveal in this book***. I have learned how to make money from successful ideas and even profit from those ventures that don't go as planned.*** (I don't like to say "failed" or "loser"). Throughout my career, I have raised financing for thousands of ideas and companies. That's why I believe I can assist anyone wanting to profit in business by laying out my hard-learned **"tricks of the trade,"** from the up-and-coming entrepreneur with a bright idea, to established business owners looking to expand their company privately or publicly.

I call this book ***The Book of Secrets.*** I hope you use it as a ***textbook***, which means you will read it many times and refer back to it as your business ideas grow. When you refer back to this ***The Book of Secrets***, you will read things that may not have applied to you or your business the first time you read it. However, as your business expands, areas in this book you skipped may prove paramount to your success when you reread it. I extend my best wishes to you as you take the exciting road to entrepreneurial freedom and financial success.

What is a Master's Course In Becoming A Millionaire?

When I was 27 years old, while vacationing on my Hatteras yacht with a few clients and employees in Cabo San Lucas, Mexico, one of them asked me, "How much did your boat cost?" When I told him I got a great deal on it for under a million dollars, he responded, **"Wow, you have done well in business. What university did you graduate from?"** I have been asked this same question repeatedly throughout my business career.

I explained to my guests that I barely graduated from high school, have never attended a university, and that I obtained my business experience from a lifetime of actually being in business, taking risks, and having great mentors. My 30-year-old guest who had a master's in business (who was basically just getting by financially) responded with, "I guess instead of spending seven years in college working on a master's degree in business like I did, you spent those years actually in business earning millions of dollars. **You basically earned a master's degree in making millions,"** hence, the term, *A Master's Course In Making Millions.*

At left is the Hatteras yacht Uhuru (freedom) anchored in Mexico. This was the first of several yachts owned by the then 27-year-old Bruce Berman and the location where the term "A Master's Degree in Making Millions" was created.

"It's not what you make, it's what you keep."

I was a millionaire at age 26. In fact, I am a still a millionaire today at 46, even though I have gone through a Chapter 7 and Chapter 11 bankruptcy. When I was writing this section, my assistant, who also is my nephew, read it and said, "Uncle Bruce, I didn't know that you ever went broke."

I replied, **"I have never been broke. Bankruptcy is just another business tool you can use to make millions of dollars.** In fact, I actually kept a $2 million dollar home almost debt-free after walking out of bankruptcy court." I then looked at him and said, "Michael, let me know when you get that broke." We both laughed. Bankruptcy can put big money in your pocket if you know how to use it. That's what I call, **"when life hands you lemons, make lemonade."**

My 24-year-old nephew has worked for me only a short time, however, I recently observed him putting together a finder's fee agreement (based upon what he learned working on this book with me). This is expected to earn him a $2,000 to $4,000 a-month royalty fee, for simply introducing two parties to each other. I expect my young nephew to complete his "Master's Course In Becoming A Millionaire" soon.

What have I done?

I've been an entrepreneur since I was born. I started my first multi-million-dollar company at age 23 with a few thousand dollars supplied by a minority partner and some used office furniture I acquired by trading a commission for (I will explain how I did it in the next section). Remember, I barely graduated from high school. I came up with another business idea (in an elevator) one Thanksgiving holiday. **I wrote a business plan template that is now included in my program, "The Berman Differential"** and with it raised $1,500,000 between Christmas and Super Bowl Sunday. Four-and- a-half months after I came up with that idea, my company raised almost $4,000,000 and went public. *My stock was worth over $50,000,000 on the second day of trading. You read correctly, $50,000,000 from a 4 $1/2$–month-old idea! Would you work day and night 4 $1/2$ months if it meant $50,000,000? The logical answer is "yes."* If your answer is "no," return this book or give it to someone who wants to succeed. In this book, I will explain to you what I have done and still do to make millions of dollars.

Need ideas? This book will show you how to come up with them. Have an idea? This book will show you how to launch it the same way as someone with a Master's in Making Millions.

By using the strategies and secrets outlined in this book, I have earned millions of dollars for my partners and myself. I have actively assisted thousands of companies secure financing in more industries than I can recount. The tools I have learned in my 46 years as a self-made entrepreneur and millionaire are explained here in an easy-to-follow format.

Sincerely,

Bruce A. Berman

Bruce A. Berman

PART ONE
{ My Master's Course in Making Millions }

This section provides you with some background about how and where I developed the skills and knowledge in business that I intend to pass on to you. This book is packed with secret (until now) business strategies and many hard-earned business lessons that will help you make, and more importantly, keep more money.

Each part, section, subsection, and page in this book may have a specific heading or topic that may not be of interest to you at this time. I can't stress enough the importance of reading this book cover-to-cover and in order. Pages with headings in this book that may not apply to you right now contain business secrets and strategies that will be of much benefit to your long-term financial success.

Learning the Secrets and Strategies of a Self-Made Millionaire

As an accomplished self-made entrepreneur and businessman, I have had the pleasure and task of tackling, surviving, and conquering a lifetime of challenges, which have shaped me as a person, developed me as a capitalist, and held a favorable influence on my pocketbook. When I look back at the millions and millions of dollars I earned in business transactions over the years, I not only have experienced joy from the fruits of my labor, but I have the bittersweet satisfaction of knowing that I made all that money with a low C-average high-school education.

In this book, I have reduced my life's most valuable assets to writing about what I learned along the way. The lessons, strategies, and guidelines gained from my experiences can guide you through the challenging and rewarding road to financial freedom.

If you already have a profitable, established business, good for you, but keep reading. I have given business advice to some of the world's leading business owners. As we were smoking cigars in the kitchen of my house, I discussed telecommunications strategies with the co-founder of Broadcom, who is a billionaire. I don't know what it is about kitchens and me, but while discussing business strategies on a pending transaction in the kitchen of one of the largest shareholders of Dow Jones Inc., I was told that I had a brilliant business mind.

This book details a lifetime of my most valuable financial lessons and business techniques. They will give you an edge in developing or expanding your business, if you choose to use them. I learned the lessons outlined here as a young entrepreneur, which have created the foundation on which I built multi-million dollar deals and businesses with.

So, if you are anywhere between a beginner and a billionaire, the lessons I have learned can help you make and keep more money.

I can't recall how many times I have heard beginners say, ***"I can't make million dollar deals. I don't have much money."*** It's not true! The average person thinks that rich people get rich out of luck. The idea that hard work and research have anything to do with it rarely crosses their minds. Many believe the reason they are not rich and never will be is because they have convinced themselves they are not worthy of being rich. In order to begin to develop a financially strong business, you must allow yourself to understand the simplicity of money.

I began to learn this lesson when one of my rich mentors said, ***"The only difference between $10,000 deals and $1,000,000 deals is two zeros,"*** and ***"When you deal in million-dollar deals, the droppings make you rich."*** What's amazing is the simplicity of putting together million-dollar deals. Basically, ***I molded and transformed the same fundamentals I learned in the beginning of my business career into a cohesive system in order to complete large transactions.***

Pay close attention to the lessons and stories in this chapter even though they start out as tiny transactions; the business skills I acquired from them has netted millions of dollars. Remember, I didn't go to college, so my ability to put together million dollar deals was obtained solely from actual business transactions, both profitable and unprofitable, and ***not making the same unprofitable decision twice.*** (Some people call "unprofitable" deals mistakes. I believe that it is only a mistake if you do the same thing more than once—the first time is part of your education.) Using the tools laid out in this book and in my program, "The Berman Differential," will help you avoid some of my costly lessons.

There are lessons in everything we do in life. ***If we learn from a***

business deal that did not go the way we intended we have an opportunity to learn how to make more money and fewer errors. **We must also learn how not to "leave money on the table"** when things are going well. It is a very common error when a business venture is going well to overlook many areas where profits can substantially be increased. **The lessons in the following short stories deal with a variety of issues relating to Perceived Value, Endorsements, Reinvesting your Profits, Outsourcing, Contracts, Added Value, Greed**, and **OPM (Other People's Money).** I will elaborate on these areas later in the book.

Everyone wants to do business with a winner. If you are not a winner, find one and put him to work for you. My first venture into the business world was with a product called "Creepy People." I had a toy that made little plastic-like figurines that attached to pencils. I was 10 years old when I approached a popular classmate and told him if he would put one of my Creepy People on each of his pencils at school, and tell everyone that they were cool, I would pay him .05 for each one I sold. This is what is referred to as an **endorsement.** My little scheme netted me $25. I took that $25 to a product surplus store where I bought yo-yos that had a pre-printed price of .99, and bought them for .20 each. This is called **reinvesting your profits.** The yo-yos had a **perceived value** of almost $1. I went back to the same popular kid, who was more than eager to do business with me again because we had established a profitable relationship, and **everyone wants to do business with a winner** (or at least someone they believe is a winner). **I sold my yo-yos for .75 each because they had a perceived value of $1.** I had successfully parlayed $25 into almost $100.

Don't let yourself get boxed in

When I was in elementary school, my neighbor worked for a major toy company. His son had every new toy he desired. I wanted a new five-speed bike with a gear changer that looked like a car stick shift that I saw in my neighbor's catalog. It cost $80, which was a lot of money in the 60s.

I went to my neighbor and signed the order for my new bike and gave him $80 in cash. I waited three weeks for my bike to arrive. During the time I was waiting for the bike, I convinced my parents to let me get a paper route, even though I was only 12 years old. I was scheduled to start the route one week after my new bike was to arrive. I didn't want to deliver 80 papers on my single-speed Stingray bike because my route had a lot of hills to climb. When the bike came, it had an entirely different shifter than what I ordered or wanted. I got upset and told my neighbor I needed my bike now and I wanted it the way it was in the picture. He told me the company had upgraded the shifter and discontinued the one I ordered. Then he pulled out my order and read me the part where it said the company had the option to deliver products with upgraded features. ***I didn't have a choice. I was in a box,*** because I needed the five speeds for the paper route and I couldn't wait for another bike.

I accepted the bike that was sent to me but learned a lesson:, ***read the fine print in contracts***. Another valuable lesson I learned was to have backup plans—also known as ***running parallel paths.*** If I hadn't paid for the bike in full, I could have walked from the order, lost a small deposit, and bought a different bike.

If you want the job done right, you can't do it all yourself

I got paid $1 a day extra to fold the newspapers I was to deliver. Now, there were a lot of younger kids who weren't old enough to get such a prestigious job as paperboy, so I hired them to fold the papers at a fraction of what I was being paid. This is called ***Outsourcing***. Today, businesses outsource many services that used to be done internally.

Creating added value

In my senior year of high school (1975), I began to work for two guys in the van customizing business. Basically, they installed carpet, wood paneling, beds, and iceboxes into new vans. After working for this company a while, I noticed that even though the van conversions were sold to an auto dealer at a profit of about $500, the real profit was in selling the completed package. I estimated that the auto dealer who brought us the vans to convert marked them up an additional $2,000, *creating added value.*

Since I knew how to convert the vans, and I found out where the car dealers were buying and selling them, I decided I would get into that business, known as *knocking off a winner*. I was about to graduate from high school and turn 18. I found out that I could get a used car dealer license at 18 if I had an office and a place to park two cars. I noticed the two partners for whom I worked were having disagreements. I went to the partner I liked the most and approached him with my idea. A few months later we were partners. We bought one used van at a wholesale car auction, did our standard van conversion, and sold the van retail for a handsome profit. We were *creating added value* by purchasing a product, adding a feature, and selling the completed package. We had several profit centers; we made money when we bought the car wholesale, installed the interior, and sold it retail, instead of wholesale.

Then I got greedy and tried to do too many vans at one time. I decided that I would use the *wrong kind of OPM (Other People's Money)*. Because I sold retail automobiles I was entrusted by the state to withhold sales tax and pay it quarterly to the government. This obligation amounted to a fairly substantial sum of money. I floated those funds to acquire more vehicles. Before I knew it, I had 10 vans being converted at once. Like many beginning entrepreneurs, I was lousy at paperwork.

The state audited me and found that I had inadvertently dipped into my sales tax reserves and was assessed large penalties and fines. ***This is where I learned the valuable lesson of not making the same mistake twice.*** This led to an audit by the Department of Motor Vehicles and the revocation of my auto dealer license for keeping poor records. I decided to liquidate my inventory and tools, and after I paid everyone off, I still had some cash leftover and a nice personal vehicle. I decided to venture into a new career.

Never leave money on the table

I got a part-time job as a messenger for a finance company, and signed up for a few classes at a local junior college. I remember one of the classes was a marketing class, or shall I say sales? I learned two valuable things in that class: ***those who can, do; and those that can't, teach; and never ask a question in sales that can be answered with a no.***

That's what I got out of my short stint at a junior college. Don't get me wrong. If you have a college education, good for you. I just believe you don't need one to become a millionaire.

I was still working as a messenger, getting paid just above minimum wage and reimbursed for mileage. Life was simple; I was always in a good mood and when I delivered my packages, usually to the same places, customers were always glad to see me. Business was picking up at the finance company, and I was taking on more and more responsibility. I was taught to run and evaluate credit, do collection calls, perform data entry, and then I became a salesman. I had two major duties as a salesman: convince companies that sold equipment to have their clients use my company to finance their purchases, and convince the people I used to drop off packages to (the lenders), to approve the loans, and approve them quickly.

Now, since I had such a good rapport with the lenders from my messenger days, they gave me special service. ***Some people don't like to burn bridges. I agree that you need to build them, as you might need them later.*** I quickly advanced and became sales manager, then vice-president of marketing, and then vice-president of the company. On the way up, I learned to ***be nice to the little people.*** I sold because people liked me. I got my work done fast because I treated everyone like they were the president of the company.

I went to the president of my company, who had taken me under his wing, much like how I am taking you under mine, on several occasions and asked for, and received, a bigger percentage of the sale. The last time I went to him, I pointed out that we made a substantial profit on leases when they expired because of the residual value of the equipment. I asked him for a percentage of that profit. He agreed I deserved it. I said to him, "I thought you were my mentor. I have worked here for four years and not until I asked about the back-end profit did you mention it." He responded, ***"I was teaching you a valuable lesson—never to leave money on the table."*** Since then I have always looked at all business ventures to see where all the profit centers are and where they could be further developed.

Build the illusion of instant credibility

After reaching as high as I could at that company, I decided to start a new company with a partner. I went to my old partner in the van business and made a deal with him: 55% for me, 45% for him. I had the knowledge and the business contacts; he had cash and was a very hard worker. In lieu of part of my severance pay from my previous employer, I bartered for some office equipment and furniture. My partner put up cash, and we were in business.

One Newport Place, 9th floor, Newport Beach, California, a well-known building in Southern California, was our business headquarters. Choosing this location was a tactic called **building the illusion.** Our prestigious address lent us credibility.

Even though we were merely a startup, our stationery and business cards, with our lofty address printed on them, gave the impression of an established business. No one had to know that our office was a small space in a large building, in which four people were crammed.

Create an image and assume that all salesmen are liars

Image is important, especially when you are selling a service. We quickly generated a brochure, which was basically a list of my past achievements carefully crafted to give the appearance that our new company had a track record. We weighed the brochure package and found it would cost about $3.50 to mail out. I wanted to get thousands of them out, but mailing them was not cost effective or an assurance that the proper person would receive the packages.

We hired two salesmen on a commission basis. Back then the prevailing draw to pay a salesman was about $1,000. We figured anybody could make approximately 25 stops a day, drop off a brochure, and get a person's card where they had been. **We made them get a card to prove they showed up.** Twenty-five deliveries a day equaled 125 a week and 500 a month. The result was that we got our packages hand-delivered along with getting business cards and receiving a written report for only $2 a package, which was cheaper than mail. We went through many salesmen to find the best ones. After a salesman would leave, we sent a new one to the same places the old one went. This gave the appearance that we had a large sales force, which gave us more credibility.

That company, which was started with under $10,000 and some office furniture, grew into a $10,000,000 company in two years. I will never forget sitting down with my old partner on our 2-year business anniversary and he said, ***"Can you believe we started this $10,000,000 company with under $10,000?"*** I replied, ***"We just didn't start a company with under $10,000; we started a $10,000,000 finance company with under $10,000."***

There were a lot of things I learned during my tenure in the finance industry. Just a few of them were how to get ***commercial financing, bank financing, learn what industries were hot, what makes a business succeed, and most importantly, what makes a business not go as planned.***

The Science of Starting a $200 Million Company

"When opportunity knocks, grab it before it goes away." In my line of work, I look at a lot of interesting business opportunities. In the 80s, I considered financing for the wind energy business. This particular industry was fueled by lucrative tax incentives for everyone involved, and a government mandate for power companies to buy all the power these windmills produced at a premium. After investigating the industry for financing, I decided to start a wind energy company. I believed there was a short ***window of opportunity*** because the tax incentives were soon to expire.

I sold my interest in the finance company to my former partner, and hooked up with a different partner. My new partner whose specialty was doing large project financings, and we formed a wind energy company. ***In business, you are as good as the way you present your last deals' success.*** Having earned the nickname "the spin doctor," my last deals were a success and I have no trouble attracting partners, investors and strategic business alliances. ***Not wanting to use our own money, we invested $50,000 that we borrowed from a local bank.*** Why were we able to borrow $50,000 and start a wind energy business? Because I implemented the lessons I have laid out in this book.

Windmills were in great demand because of the lucrative tax credits available. We pre-sold our first project of a 40-unit wind project, which equated to about $5,000,000 ($125,000 each). **We built that project with "mirrors."** We used the $50,000 credit line to open an office, make brochures, and put a deposit down on some land in the Palm Springs area to build the first 40 units. When we had the first 10 units sold, we collected $250,000 in deposits. When we deposited the $250,000 (OPM) in the bank, we gained credibility. We then were able to convince the manufacturer that we could pay for the product because we had the orders financed. Essentially, we used the bank's $50,000 to get started and our customers' $250,000 in deposits to order the equipment we sold.

After our first project's success, we expanded the business. Using the old business philosophy of **"controlling your own destiny"** (remember the bike incident? —I had no choice but to rely on one source), we grew the business by starting our own construction company to build the concrete and electrical infrastructure, purchased our own NASD-licensed securities firm to sell the products, and ultimately purchased the manufacturer of the windmills. Our companies grew fast. **The combined entities employed over 200 people and were responsible for over a quarter of a billion dollars of windmills built and sold.** After two years in that business, I had grown a personal net worth (according to a personal financial statement prepared by Deloitte, Haskins and Sells, now known as Deloitte & Touche) of over $20,000,000.

At 27 years old Bruce Berman purchased this brand new custom mansion from its builder in the exclusive community of Nellie Gail Ranch in Laguna Hills, California. A few hundred yards away, after becoming a billionaire, Broadcom's cofounder purchased a similar home built by the same builder.

Subsequently, I learned many more lessons: ***growing pains, due diligence, mergers, international finance, bank failures, insurance claims, lawsuits, and bankruptcy.***

In order to protect our financial position we decided to acquire the manufacturer of the windmills we were selling. This decision ultimately led to a tremendous financial learning experience. When we acquired that company, we acquired its problems. If memory serves me correct, they had sold approximately 2,000 windmills, which, in turn, were sold for over $200,000,000. A major insurance company had guaranteed the performance and energy production of those windmills. Well, guess what? All of those windmills developed an engineering defect that caused them to malfunction. This defect was designed in the machine years before we bought the machines and the company. The insurance company decided not to honor their claim. The potential loss was too large and the insurance carrier basically said to sue them. At the same time, a major bank that financed our customers was shut down by the FDIC. Since most of our customers financed their purchases there was approximately $10,000,000 of our customers' loan proceeds due us in transit. The FDIC was not interested in funding new loans and unwound all those loans, causing us an unforeseen cash crunch. The federal government let the tax credits expire, which were the incentive behind the sales of the windmills.

Now, any one of those was a big obstacle to deal with, but all of those within the same few months caused our company to seek protection under Chapter 11 Bankruptcy. *Ultimately, I personally was forced into an involuntary Chapter 7 Bankruptcy, which I cleverly converted to a Chapter 11. After several years of fighting legal battles in many courtrooms, I learned more about business from this situation than from any other venture in my life. I forgot to mention that the IRS sued me for $21,000,000, and my partner passed away during the ordeal. I was only 28 years old. So what was the conclusion to this challenging bowl of lemons? My company was reorganized and I personally discharged all lawsuits and debts (except I settled with the IRS for $300,000), and got to keep my nearly paid off $2,000,000 house.*

As I have previously stated, if you learn from business ventures that do not go as planned, you are a winner. My mentor used to say to me, *"It's not how much you make, but how much you keep." My net worth rose to $20,000,000 during that venture; however, I only kept my home in Texas.* Protecting assets is a key lesson for any successful businessperson. The time to plan and protect yourself is in the beginning stage of the business.

"Never try to beat a man at his own game." If I've heard this adage that once, I've heard it a thousand times. From windmills, I decided to switch gears and get in the oil and gas and Arabian horse businesses. After all, I was living in Texas. I purchased some existing oil wells for which I paid a small premium for because I wanted to get started in business in Texas. I also bought an Arabian horse through the realtor who sold my house to me in Texas. Well, lucky for me, the price of oil shot up and I was able to sell the wells that I had overpaid for at a profit. The horse was another expensive piece of my "Master's Course In Becoming A Millionaire." The bottom line is, I knew nothing about horses or oil wells; *I did not do proper*

Due Diligence, and that caused me to lose money on the horse and not make as much as I could have made in oil wells.

If I would have done proper due diligence, I would have learned more about the costs associated with running an oil well. Ironically, one of the most costly factors in the monthly operation of an oil well is disposing of excess water that is pumped up with the oil. My neighbor in Texas used to call horses "hay-eaten sons-of-bitches." Need I say more? Due Diligence.

After licking my wounds from Texas once my bankruptcy was over, I decided to sell my ranch and move back to California. There I met my future wife, who happened to be a Playboy Playmate, actress, and model. I had two children at the time from a previous marriage. My teenage daughter wanted to go to modeling school and asked me for $1,000. When I mentioned this to my current wife, she looked at me and said, "I can teach her everything she needs to know about modeling in 30 minutes." Within seconds, I came up with the idea of making a video on how girls could become models called "Modeling Made Easy." Here I had my ducks lined up. My wife was a fairly famous model and could write the script, do the casting, and be the star. We put together a budget, researched how much videos sold for, how much it would cost to duplicate and produce. I did my **Due Diligence.** I like to say every successful businessman is an **Opportunist**. I saw an opportunity to use the full potential of assets in my reach, and I used them. **Many people have business opportunities at their fingertips and let them fall by the wayside. Don't be this person.** Use the tools in this program as your guide and be your own success story. **Nothing ventured, nothing gained**. My video, more than 10 years later, still is being sold for $35.95 each, when they cost only a few dollars to copy. What business opportunities are in front of you? Who do you know who has an idea or a business that you can expand?

Earning Over $50,000,000 in 4¹/₂ Months

From my video enterprise, I dabbled in real estate. My lifestyle was quickly depleting my cash reserves. My wife and I had expensive automobiles (a Rolls Royce, Porsche, and an SUV) and lived in an exclusive area in Encino, California near the Jackson family compound. One day I ran into an old associate of mine and when he asked what I was doing for a living and I told him I was supporting myself from the video revenues and my savings. He told me he had made millions of dollars in his new business, which was taking companies public. I was reminded of the saying, ***"Everyone likes a winner."*** Obviously he was a winner and I appeared to be doing well and had a solid track record of putting together million dollar deals, so we reached an agreement, and I began to work for his firm. I loved the business from the get-go. My experiences were commensurate for the job. I lasted about 30 days. Both of us were strong leaders and clashed. I left and joined a competitive firm. They hired me based on my **List of Qualifications**. I am a chameleon. I will be who I need to be.

My first deal with this firm was one of its most profitable. Using my past lessons in financing, I quickly began to negotiate for a percentage of the profits. **You do not get what you are worth. You get what you negotiate.** I started at 5%, then 12 ¹/₂%, and ultimately 17 ¹/₂%. I learned the business fast and decided to do what I do best: go off on my own and start my own company. I used my last three deals as my track record. In most businesses, **you're as good as your last deal or sale.**

After raising millions of dollars for my clients' companies and taking them public, I decided it was **time to do it for myself**. I wrote a business plan/offering **(using the format in "The Berman Differential" program)** over one Thanksgiving to raise $1,000,000 to launch my own public company. The offering did so well I raised $1,500,000 over Christmas vacation. FYI; between Thanksgiving and Super Bowl Sunday (in mid January) is historically the worst time of year to raise money, so I was pleased with the immediate acceptance of my business plan and offering. I truly believe that because of the format I used in that business plan, which is available to you, I was able to convey all the necessary information to investors in a very easy-to-follow document. This cut down on confusing the investors and allowed them to actually enjoy reading the document rather than turning them off with unrealistic business plans that are prepared by parties that only know how to write them but have never funded one in their life. On April 7th, the company went public, which was just over four months from idea stage. On April 10th, the second day of trading, my company's stock closed at $7.25 per share. I had 8,000,000 shares. $7.25 times 8,000,000 shares = **$58,000,000. Not bad for 4 $1/2$ months of work.**

PART TWO
{ The ABC's of **A**ctually **B**eginning a **C**ompany }

Not only have I started numerous businesses for myself, I have assisted thousands of companies in their startup phase. In this section, I explain how to form and structure a company, create an image, analyze a potential business idea, purchase an existing company, or start your own.

Even if you already own a business, this section is useful in expanding your business and growth potential and increasing your profits.

Analyzing a Potential Business Opportunity or Franchise

About last night

Recently my sister called me and said she was planning to borrow some money to start a franchise business and asked if I would analyze the opportunity for her. My sister and I are business and academic opposites. She earned a master's degree in communications, taught at three universities, and has been an employee at Fortune 500 companies most of her life. I, unlike my sister, am a self-taught businessman with no formal education.

When my sister announced her intentions, I was a week away from sending the draft of this book to her for feedback. I realized that my book did not directly address her needs, so I decided to add this section, and that instead of analyzing the business opportunity for her, I would let her read this section and see if she could answer her own questions. Now, since you are reading this book, this section obviously worked for her or she would have edited it out.

The "Bermanator"

Throughout my career, I have developed the ability to analyze businesses, find their holes, weed out the over-zealous management claims, and shred their business plans. This is how I got my nickname "The Bermanator." While it may not seem flattering, it is mandatory in business to be able to effortlessly dissect business opportunities.

I developed an opening statement that makes my questioning seem less offensive. It goes like this, "Mr. Smith, I must ask some questions that may seem invasive, unnecessary, and even like I don't know what I am talking about. Keep in mind, I am only asking these questions because I know my investors or partners will ask me to answer these questions, and I want to know the answers before they are asked."

In my next section on buying a business, I will explore specific questions to ask when buying a business and other tips in analyzing a potential business.

The Franchise

According to IFA's Franchise Opportunities Guide, ***"one out of every three dollars spent by Americans for goods or services is spent in a franchised business."*** Franchises are much easier to analyze than most businesses mainly because the franchisor is required to disclose business events that other businesses may not have to disclose. The first thing to do is request a copy of the franchise document. In most documents there will be a list of current franchises and even recently terminated franchises. Pick up the phone and call them or drive by and visit them. You would be surprised how people like to brag or complain about their businesses. Here are a few questions for current franchise owners.

1. **Are you happy with your franchise? If you had it to do over again, would you buy the same franchise or another? If the franchisee is not happy or wouldn't do it all over again, consider it a red flag.**

2. **Was the training thorough, how long was it, and did you like it? If you are not properly trained, your chances of failing skyrocket.**

3. **Are the franchise fees you are paying the same as your interpretation of the agreement, or are they more? Some salespeople twist words and try to paint a rosy picture and skip over hidden costly fees.**

4. **What type of business experience did you have before purchasing the franchise? If they had more experience than you and are having a tough time, what makes you think you would be different? If they have less**

experience than you and are very successful, that is a great sign.

5. Were there any hidden franchise fees or unexpected costs? It's the unexpected that gets you every time.

6. Did the franchisor estimate the amount of operating cash you would need correctly or did they underestimate? Some franchisors want you to have ample cash reserves so your chances of success are greater (which protects their brand) but there are those who just want to sell franchises and are not necessarily worried if you fail or not.

7. Is your territory big enough to hit your goals? Too small of a territory will limit your upside, and we are all in business for the upside.

8. Does the franchisor advertise as much as they said they would? One of the main reasons to buy a franchise is for its brand identity. If the franchisor doesn't advertise as much as they say they will, it will hurt your long-term growth plans.

9. Did you hit your goals? The bottom line is, if they didn't hit their goals, it had to do with one of the above questions.

Many franchisors list the names of franchisees that left the franchisor. I would call them next. Get a feel from the current franchisees how happy they are and then use the same questions as above to gauge how the previous franchisees rate the franchisor. I also would ask a few other questions. Ex-franchisees tend to get irritated with the franchisor and are usually very willing to talk to you and to ruin a potential sale for the franchisor. Try to get past the person's anger and find out the heart of the problem. If they say, "They're crooks, I hate them," you are not getting any information. Dig in and ask more questions.

1. **Why did you leave the franchisor? The best way to find out what potential issues are is to find out from someone who's been there.**

2. **If you are still in business, are you doing better without being a franchise? Frequently business owners will leave a franchisor. It could be for a variety of reasons. In some cases the business owner has built up a loyal customer base and in others the franchise was a bad concept. Find out why and it will help you with your decision.**

3. **What should I look out for if I buy a franchise? Who better to give you the scoop than a previous owner.**

4. **If you were going to buy a franchise from a different franchisor, in the same industry, which one should they pick and why? Sometimes business owners like the industry they are in but find out other franchises offer a better deal and more profits.**

5. **Did the franchisor make any statements or representations you feel are untrue or overstated? If they lied to them, they will lie to you.**

6. **Do you like the business you are in or do you think it is a bad industry? Being in the right industry is very important.**

7. **What other industries do you like for franchises? This will give you an idea of other ways or places you could make money.**

8. **Do they want to sell your business cheap? This finds out if their complaining was true.**

There are things to interpret from the franchise document itself. Here are the areas I dig into first.

1. **What is the business experience of the franchisor management? Are they new to the business or franchise industry veterans? Do they have experience in customer support or are they all salespeople? If the management is heavy on the marketing side, you can expect to be sold. If the management is heavy on the industry side, you can expect good customer support and new products.**

2. **Is this a company that has a patented product or a trademark that is well known and instills quality? Patents and trademarks are what keep a business going for many years.**

3. **Are they in litigation with their franchisees or anyone claiming rights to their product? If so, does it appear to be a reasonable amount for the number of franchisees they have? One per 50 would be average.**

4. **What type of restrictions do they put on your business? Be careful they don't regulate everything you do.**

5. **If you want to sell your franchise, what is the process and what are the costs involved? Imagine you want to sell your franchise and when you turn back to your contract it says the franchisor gets a fee on the sale. Know what you're getting into upfront; read and study the fine print.**

6. **How do they protect your territory? That is one of the most important things you are buying.**

7. **Can you sell other products or do you have to sell and use only theirs? For example, if you bought a suntan franchise, can you sell lotions and bathing suits?**

The franchisor's financial statements should be enclosed in the offering document. They are a wealth of information. Read them and understand them. Show them to an accountant friend if you don't understand accounting.

1. **Is the franchisor making money? If they are not doing well, how are you expected to do well?**

2. **Where is their profit? Is it selling franchises or selling products to the franchisees? I would prefer to see the majority of their profit in selling products to franchisees. That at least gives an indication that the franchisor is devoted to you selling products.**

3. **What is their profit margin on the products they sell you? If they are severely marked up, it will make the price you have to charge to sell the products tougher to compete with against a non-franchise.**

4. **Does the company reinvest money in product development and enhancements? That would lend credibility to their belief that the product has long-term viability.**

5. **Divide their gross product revenue by the number of stores they have and you will see what an average store buys in products. Then compare that to the amount they suggest you will sell in their sales materials.**

Here are some basic business examining tactics

First of all, even if you are not buying a franchise, the preceding information is a basic outline for examining a business opportunity. There are many other things to consider before making the vital plunge into business ownership. *I am an optimistic realist. I expect the best and prepare for the worst.*

1. **After analyzing the cash needs for the business, do you**

have enough cash available to live on if the business doesn't make any money? Don't put yourself in a position that if you have a few bad months, you have to close or sell the business.

2. If you intend to use investor money, are you planning on taking a salary out of the company before it is profitable? Investors don't like that. Typically investors like to see the business making a profit and the investors beginning to get a return before you start paying yourself.

3. If the business takes off, are you committed to putting in long hours? If not, forget it You do not have the work ethic needed to own a franchise.

4. If the business grows, are you willing to put everything on the line to build a thriving business? Some people do not prepare for things to go well. If your business takes off, you are going to want to expand and that means more risk. Be prepared to be successful. If you don't, you are a loser going into the deal.

5. Do you know people who can help you get started, i.e., customers or potential staff in the area?

6. Are you a likable upbeat person? If you are a depressed, low-energy person, customers will not want to come into your business. You need to exude confidence and cheer.

7. Is the industry you're going into up-and-coming or dying out? I can remember when suntan booths were a thriving industry and opening at a phenomenal rate. Then came all the public concern about the negative effects of ultraviolet rays and skin cancer, and the momentum came to a halt.

8. **Do you or your family have experience in the industry? If you can draw from a pool of people you know and trust to help you, your chances of success increase.**

9. **How are you with rejection? Better get used to it.**

Opening a business is an adrenaline rush. There is nothing more exciting than opening your first business. If you can open a business, you are a winner. Whether or not the first business you open succeeds or doesn't make as much money as planned, you're a winner. Once you learn how to open a business, you will always know how to open a business.

The trick is to make money off the hot ones while you can. Learn from the not-so-hot ones and don't make the same mistake twice. Using the tools laid out in this book and my program, "The Berman Differential," you will learn how to use other people's money to open your own businesses. There are always people willing to invest in the right idea, packaged correctly at the right time.

Instant Up: Basic Consulting

Not a consultant? Maybe you should be!

If you're not a consultant, this chapter will show you how to easily earn consulting income. Finders' fees are common tools to earn money by just putting two people together. Many of you who may already earn your living by being consultants can pick up a few tips here, too.

How do I become a consultant?

Do you have a talent or can you provide a service someone or some company needs? In today's economy, more businesses are looking to outside service providers (consultants) to resolve their business needs. Outsourcing has been growing rapidly since the mid 1990s. Why? It saves them time and money and increases their profits.

Most businesses have several areas where they need staff, but not on a full-time basis. Businesses have a standard of quality and professionalism in their image they desire to maintain, so they won't do anything to jeopardize it. For instance, let's say a major hardware store wants to hold seminars once a week at their stores to teach people how to retile their bathrooms. They obviously do this to sell their tile products and garner customer loyalty. Now, since this store only does this once a week, it does not make economic sense to keep an instructor on the payroll full time.

Putting on the seminar is very valuable to the store, and since their image is important to them, their best solution for this situation is to hire a consultant. The consultant comes in once a week, holds the seminar, and then leaves. By hiring the consultant the company doesn't have the burden of health insurance, payroll taxes, vacation pay time, sick days, and having to keep the retile expert working the other four days a week.

Many rapidly expanding companies out to raise money have "holes in their business plans," which include positions they need to fill immediately to lend credibility to their business. Rather than entering into long-term contracts (usually involving stock and substantial head-hunter fees) with key management personnel, they may prefer to hire a consultant to fill the gap in their plan.

Who needs me to find something or someone for them?

Everyone! A definition of a finder can ***be a person who knows two people.*** It's that simple and anyone, anywhere, at any time can earn consultant and finder's fees. The best thing about it is you don't need to be a sales rep, employee, or even an associate to meet two people, and you can make deals with ***anyone***. A sales rep for a telecom company may need new clients (everyone needs new clients) and have a good product at a better price than his competitors. If you meet a person who controls the expenses for a large firm, tell him you know someone who has been saving money for similar companies, and introduce him to the telecom rep. Then you can earn a fee, and you never look like a salesperson. People never like to feel like they are being sold something. If you are a sales rep for a company, your motives are on your sleeve. If you know a person who can help someone you just met, you gain a new friend.

This has to be the simplest way anyone can create a personal revenue stream. I look for finder's fees every day and pay for them with a smile. The best way to do this is to open your eyes and ears. Talk with people you meet through friends, go to community networking events, get to know people who do credible business, and ask them if they are willing to pay referral fees if you can bring them customers. If they say no, ask them how they get new business. Most people advertise. Explain to them that paying a finder's fee could save them advertising dollars, and they only pay when they make money. Spend a few minutes explaining how, and if they don't get it, move on to the next person. Eventually, you're going to run into someone credible who is desirous of increasing his or her business. When that happens, consider that person a partner and remember him or her when you hear that someone could use your partner's services. I stress the word **hear**, because if people would open their ears more often, they would hear money where they used to hear nothing.

You've probably have heard the term, **"Money Talks."** Darn right, it does. Money will talk to you when the person with an office down the hall wants to by a new, expensive car and you know a Mercedes dealer who will pay you a finder's fee for bringing in new business. Money raises its voice when your golf buddy brings a friend who has just moved to town for a quick 18 holes and wants to know where he can find a good lawyer in the area. You refer him to one who gives you legal advice pro bono because you refer him business. And money shouts out your name and says, "take me now," when you're at a cocktail party and a woman you just meet says, "I love this area. I have been looking for a waterfront home for some time. Do you know any real estate agents who would like to sell someone a waterfront home?" I'll bet you do.

These are just examples of situations where before you made recommendations and now you make a fee.

The first rule for consultants

In the beginning of a contractual relationship between a consultant and a party desirous of hiring the consultant, the hiring party is usually anxious for the consultant to begin work and willing to pay for his services. **First rule: Get your consultant agreement in writing.** Be as specific as you can be of the scope of the services you are to perform and the compensation you are to receive.

Many parties that hire consultants perform 100% of their contractual duties to pay the consultants. Be forewarned, many parties that hire consultants default on their obligation to pay them. There are a lot of different reasons this happens. The majority of those situations I have come in contact with seem to be created by companies regretting the amount of compensation that they previously agreed to pay the consultants.

The consulting client curve

Here is a typical situation and the mentality of a company that hires a consultant. Company ABC hires consultant Smith. ABC is desperate to increase sales so they agree to pay a 20% commission to Smith for locating buyers for their products. They agree to compensate Smith the 20% for the life of any clients he brings them. Smith brings them a huge client. The client buys 50% of the products the company sells, which equates to $2,000,000 a year in sales for ABC, and $400,000 a year due Smith.

ABC is ecstatic in the beginning. Their troubles are over, sales are up, and the company is making a profit. Smith has contractually performed his duties and is earning his commissions. Now six months go by and ABC's CEO realizes Smith is earning more as a consultant than the CEO earns. The CEO gets resentful. After all, he is working 60 hours a week for $250,000 a year and Smith works a few hours a week at most and is making $400,000 a year off his company. What does the CEO do? He goes to his attorney and tries to break the contract. Sound silly? It happens all the time.

Now, it's a year down the road and the client you referred to ABC wants a better price from ABC on the products they order. They tell ABC they want a 10% reduction in price. ABC can't afford to lose the client, so where do you think they want to get that 10%? From you, the consultant.

This is what I call the consultant client curve. In the beginning, they love you because you saved the company. Then, a few months later the company starts to realize you are making a lot of money and their attitude becomes "we paid you too much." Another few months pass and they start to think "we could have done it without you." After all, ABC is doing all the work. Then comes the bomb. The client wants a price reduction and the company gets the attitude "the consultant screwed us, let's sue him."

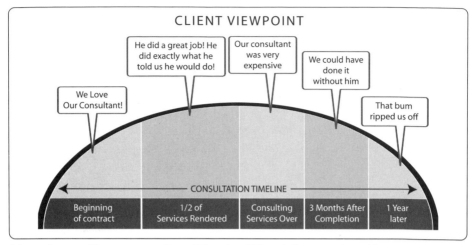

Here is another example. I had a friend (a construction worker) that came to me for free advice when he had an idea for a web-based business. I spent several hours analyzing his business plan and meeting with him. I later outlined a course of action for him and suggested he come back when he got a little further down the road. **He thanked me profusely for the advice knowing I usually don't give away my advice for free.** About a year and a half later, he came back and wanted to show me the progress he had made and wanted to see if I could help him. I was impressed that he had implemented the things I suggested.

I told him his timing was horrible to launch an Internet project because the market had dried up and that it was 10 times the work it was a year earlier to get an internet company off the ground and funded. He was persistent and basically pleaded with me to help him. Knowing that he didn't have much money to pay for my services, I agreed to accept a fraction of what I usually charge in cash, plus some options to buy stock in the company. Because he was a friend, I would only agree to a short contract. I suggested we work together and see how it went, and if we were both happy, we would renew.

In my first official meeting with the company, he had approximately 10 people march into his opulent, hi-tech conference room. They were all purported to be his employees or consultants of the company. They put on an impressive Power Point presentation on which I took notes. At the end of the presentation, I began to dig in.

First, I got to the bottom of who was who. Basically, the majority of the room consisted of people who had full time jobs elsewhere and were considering working for the company if it got funded. None of the potential employees had ever been a member of a public company's management or had ever run a business with the growth that they were projecting for my friend's company. Secondly, the company had no office space. They rented a phone line and conference room from a technology company. I opened up a new can of worms when I asked how they were going to produce their projected revenue stream. I thought their projections were grossly exaggerated. They estimated that in the next calendar year they would go from $0 to over $50,000,000 in revenues and earn almost $25,000,000; two years down the road, they projected over $200,000,000 in revenues and over $150,000,000 in profit.

Being a startup company with basically no cash, plenty of debts, with no office or tangible product prompted this question *"How did you come up with these numbers that seem so over- the- top?" The CEO looked at me with a straight face an answered "Well, in order for us to raise the amount of money we need, we had to make the projections really high or our deal wouldn't work." I started laughing hysterically and then noticed no one else in the room was laughing. The reason I laughed was because I thought he was kidding—I later found out he wasn't. They didn't get it; their exaggerated earnings statement could equal 20 years behind bars.*

The CEO and the entire staff had never before raised money in this style of transaction and were ignorant of basic security laws. When I explained how serious of a statement they had made, they were very concerned on one hand, and on the other, they were relieved I was onboard to lend expertise where it was obviously needed. The CEO had no intention of breaking any laws, however, he was a construction worker with an idea and had no experience with securities or running a large business.

I began to do what I have done time and time again for companies. I worked with the company to restructure their business plan and head them in the right direction. I showed them where they could get the business going with only $200,000. They were trying to raise several million dollars and at this startup stage and it wasn't going to happen, especially because management was trying to pay themselves over $500,000 a year in salaries. It didn't add up: raise a few million to pay a management team led by a construction worker with no experience $500,000 annually. Investment bankers don't consider this arrangement a bona fide use of proceeds. In addition, they had over a $1,000,000 allocated for a national TV commercial rollout plan. I brought in an expert who explained to them how to do a test market, spending $25,000 - $50,000 instead of the $1,000,000 that they had budgeted. I demonstrated how the business model works and focused on how the company could begin producing some revenues by targeting one sector of the market rather than half the United States, as they had planned.

As I have seen time and time again, my friend forgot whose business plan and advice they were following. When it came time to renew my contract, the company had come a long way. They had implemented all of my suggestions, raised a few hundred thousand dollars, began to produce a little revenue and were starting to

look like a real company. Unfortunately, I stepped on a lot of the employees' toes when I restructured the company. How do you think the guy who made the projections felt when I explained he had committed securities fraud or the person who wanted to spend over $1,000,000 to air a commercial without first market testing it? The tail wagged the dog and management did not renew my contract. I believe they would have successfully beat me out of my compensation had I not followed my own advice in the next section. The CEO told me I brought nothing to the table, that he did all the work. How quickly they forget.

Since I am a shareholder, I asked the CEO how well they were doing, and according to him, he was excited that they had produced a couple hundred thousand dollars in revenue. Upon asking him some specific questions, it appeared they actually had less than $100,000 in revenues. Now that's a long way from the $25,000,000 they were projecting. Good thing for him, he pulled their prior offering with those ridiculous projections or he would have been in serious trouble.

The second rule! How not to get cheated out of what you are due.

There are many things you can do to protect yourself as a consultant.

1. **Make sure your contract is airtight. Fully explain the services you are to provide and the compensation you are due. Companies that need your services will, of course, sign a contract that says they will pay you at the beginning. It's just later that they will squawk.**

2. **Document key events in writing. As you reach milestones of your agreement, get the contracting company to sign an acknowledgment that you have performed your duties. Example: You introduce them to client DEF. Have them sign a simple acknowledgement**

that you introduced DEF to the company and any sales made to DEF will generate compensation for you.

3. Stay involved in the process. Talk to the client you referred to ABC and to ABC frequently. Find out how the relationship between ABC and the client is working. Are orders being filled, how is quality control, is the client paying for their goods, is the client looking for a different supplier to sell them product, etc.

4. When you earn your first fee, no matter how small it is, collect it as soon as possible. It begins to document the fact that you are to earn fees in the future on a particular client. I just collected a $90 fee on a test market for a product that will pay me thousands of dollars each month. Why did I push for the $90 check? To get them used to paying me.

5. Be willing to negotiate and be prepared to reduce your fees in the future on sweetheart deals. Take the example above where the client asks for a price reduction from ABC Company. ABC is going to look to cut the consultant fees first. Use the win-win philosophy. If all three of you give a little and no one caves in all the way, you can walk away with money in your pocket. This is almost guaranteed to happen. Just be prepared for it, and practice what I explain in the chapter on Contract Negotiating.

Fringe Benefits of being a consultant

Besides things such as making your own hours, you are your own boss, and it's a great way to make money, there are other economic benefits to being a consultant. Check with your accountant on expenses you can either write off fully or partially on your income taxes.

1. **Travel expense.** Most consultants need to travel, which also includes those trade shows and conventions that usually take place in phenomenal locations like Las Vegas, Hawaii, New York City, etc.

2. **Meals.** Did you take a client to dinner? How about for drinks? Did you go to lunch with an employee or customer?

3. **Entertainment.** Did you go golfing or to a play with a client?

4. **Business equipment.** Do you work out of your house? I have a complete office set up at home, as well as Internet service I use for business.

5. **Cell phone.** With the amount of time I spend on my cell phone, I am glad it's for business.

Get the picture? As a consultant, you become your own business and a host of deductions await you that might not otherwise be available to you. Make sure, consult an accountant, and ask him to explore all potential areas that you can benefit by tax wise for being a consultant.

How to: Actually Begin a Company When You Don't Have Any Ideas

There are Several Ways to Begin a Business

Don't worry if you don't have any money because later in this book I will tell you how to get money for business ideas. In the last section, I explained how to become a consultant. I reviewed how introducing two people basically puts you in business and allows you to earn fees and take advantage of writing off expenses. If you haven't read that section, go back and read it. In this section, I will explain other ways to start or own a business from scratch, ***even if you don't have any ideas.***

Purchasing someone else's business

One of the easiest ways to get into business is to buy someone else's business. There are always people who want to sell their businesses. It is just a matter of finding a potential seller at an opportune time. Finding the right seller, like most things in life, is a numbers game. If you attempt to put 100 deals together, you will get at least one. If you never attempt to put a deal together, you will get, at the most, none.

Each day, everywhere you go, there are possibilities of buying a business, whether you go to lunch at a restaurant, get gas at a gas mart, buy a toy for your child, do your laundry at a Laundromat, pick up your dry cleaning, get your car washed, buy flowers for your wife, develop film of the grandkids, have a family portrait taken, use a suntan booth, work out at a gym, pick up a cappuccino, buy some donuts, get a wrench at a hardware store, buy a book at the book store on how to fix your car, business opportunities abound.

Be friendly, talk to the business owners and employees and see how their businesses are doing. Find out if they are interested in selling. Small businesses are bought and sold frequently and many times they are owner financed. *Knowledge is king. The more knowledge you get, the richer you will be.* You have nothing to lose if you talk to business owners, you get what you went there for in the first place, but you may walk out with knowledge about that specific business or industry, business in the geographical in general, and who is willing to sell and who is not.

The internet is full of websites where businesses are listed for sale. However, business brokers also list on these sites and using their services will cost you more money. Let's say a seller wants to net $200,000 for his business and he wants $20,000 down and would carry a note for $180,000 in order to sell that business. If you approached him on your own, that would be the price. However, if you went through a business broker, the seller may have to pay a 15% fee on the sale to the broker. The seller then will mark that business up to $240,000 and require $60,000 down instead of $20,000 down ($40,000 to cover the broker's 15% commission and $20,000 for the seller). Now, do you see the benefit of locating a business by yourself? That extra $40,000 in cash could be used to expand the business or buy an additional company.

There are some advantages of using a reputable and knowledgeable business broker, such as in the documentation of the transaction. Although I find it more cost effective to have an attorney do the documentation for a fraction of the cost of using a business broker. After all, the attorney will document things in your favor if you hire him, and the broker will most likely cover his- or herself.

How to purchase a business

"Oh, it is a cash business. That is why our books don't show a profit [wink, wink]," says the seller. If the seller's books show they aren't making a profit, assume they aren't making a profit. It is hard to go back and claim misrepresentation to a seller when he shows you upfront that the company is not making a profit. Those types of businesses also have potential liabilities that could blow up on you later, like trouble with the IRS. A good rule is to look at all of the company's books to check if its revenue and assets are overstated and its liabilities are understated and go from there. That way, you know the worse case and any upside is in your favor.

I like to look at each business I purchase as one that can run without me. Therefore, controls need to be able to be put in place that ensure all transactions are posted to deter employees from stealing. I like the method of some retail restaurants offering you a free meal if the cashier does not give you a receipt. A business where the seller implies money is being made off the books makes it a difficult business to run as an absentee owner. However, if you're planning on running the business with just your family and never growing to multiple locations, that type of business is an option.

Many sellers will finance the sale of their business. It usually is to their tax advantage to finance the sale, especially if they are planning to retire. Here is where Negotiating 101 is useful. I prefer not to personally guarantee loans. There are viable reasons to tell a seller why you want the business to be on the financial hook. You need to preserve your available credit to expand the business and for potential operating capital needs, buying another store, etc. I would turn it around on the seller, look at him and say, "Why are you worried that the business will not make it? Is there something you are not telling me?"

If you can't get seller financing, and you still want to buy the business, your choices are using your cash if you have it, borrowing from a bank, or raising money to acquire the business from investors. There are chapters in this book that further explain the ins-and-outs of how to raise money or get bank financing.

The difference between a business owner and a non-business owner is that a business owner is someone willing to take a risk. The trick is to limit the amount of exposure you have in any given transaction and that is why I am explaining how to minimize your risks.

Why purchase an existing business?

Purchasing an existing business has its benefits. Hindsight is 20/20. When you purchase an existing business, you get the added benefit of being able to look at past performance. The trick is to see if your ideas can improve the business. Let's say you purchase a local drycleaners that is making a profit. You thoroughly examine the business and see that the equipment you own and our staff are capable of cleaning an additional $10,000 a month in clothes.

The problem is that the business does the same amount steadily each month. The previous owners were happy with the amount of business they were doing and did no advertising for new business. Your plan is to spend $1,500 a month to advertise, and after you research the advertising in the area, you believe your efforts will bring in the new customers needed to reach the additional $10,000 in sales.

After surveying the existing customers, you find they are willing to pay an extra $5 if you pick up and deliver their clothes. You look at the cost and see it will cost you $2 to deliver their clothes, and you estimate you will make 2,000 deliveries a month. You just increased the business profit $8,500 a month on the advertising plan and $6,000 a month on the delivery plan. Those were viable reasons to purchase an existing business.

You need to look at how you can improve upon every business. Just buying a business and keeping it "status quo" is a bad purchase. When you can increase sales with creativity, you are finding extra value the seller doesn't know he has and you're not paying for it (so don't tell them your ideas). You can thank me later.

Starting From Scratch

Starting from scratch is actually my favorite way to own a business. There is definitely a self-satisfying feeling that comes from creating something from scratch. Just as I explained in the preceding section, "How to Find a Business to Purchase," the same theory works for starting a business, just in reverse. Instead of looking for what businesses are for sale in your area, look for what is not there. What is needed in your neighborhood or in any geographical area? With the Internet, you can substantially increase your workable geographical area. Every product or service you need or want represents a business opportunity for you. Are these business owners smarter than you? I doubt it. They just took a chance. Armed with this book and the tools of my program, "The Berman Differential," you can change your future.

Earlier in this book, I explained how to set up a business. Later in the book, I will explain how to grow a business, and in the last chapter, I explain how to borrow, raise money, or take a company public. It's up to you to choose your business.

Have you ever noticed that when someone comes out with a good product or a new business idea, someone else comes out with a similar one? Why do they do that? Because it works. The old saying "if it's not broke, don't fix it" applies to starting a business. People like to follow a winner.

Franchisors can be an excellent source of business information. If you have your eye on a particular industry and know of a successful franchisor within that industry, go to their website and request a potential purchaser package. Franchisors' packages include an offering circular that discloses many facts about their business, including their financial statements, demographics, product information, legal issues, and their fees.

The next step is to call local franchises in your area, implying that you are considering opening a franchise in another area, and see if they are satisfied with their franchisor. You would be surprised how willing they are to talk. If you want more information on what franchises are out there, go to www.franchiselife.com.

What if I want to start a business that will grow to be $100 million in sales?

You better be in the right industry. William J. O'Neal, owner of *Investor Business Daily,* wrote in his best-selling book, "How to Make Money in Stocks," "Fifty percent of a stock's return comes from being in the best industry."

If you are looking to make big money, you have to stay on top of what's hot. Bill Gates didn't invent the computer; however, he had the foresight to move into a cutting edge and possessed the skills to quickly control its advancements. Sam Walton didn't come up with the idea for mass merchandising stores when he created Wal-Mart—he was in a market with a huge upside.

How do you know what's going to be the next big winner?

People are like a herd of animals, one exciting move can turn the entire bunch. Today, there seems to be a different reality dating show on every network channel. The cable channels have gotten in on the action too. There are reality shows for blind dating, group dating, dating while your friends watched, double dating, and dating while your ex-girlfriends watched. They have reality shows for everything; bachelors, bachelorettes, being stuck on an island, almost-forgotten celebrities beating the heck out of each other, you name it.

This phenomena goes far beyond reality shows. Whenever the "herd" gets stirred up, there is someone who will move with it. Not too long ago, elimination game shows were the hot thing. It seemed like *Who Wants to be a Millionaire* and *The Weakest Link* created a cult following. It works this way in every industry. Starbucks, starting off as a small coffee shop in Seattle, now is a household name. The same goes for clothing brands, matchmaking websites, and other industries that all have a hot trend.

Picking up industry trends can be as easy as reading the Wall Street Journal, turning on MSNBC, or reading the highlights in an entrepreneur magazine. Find out what's moving and "jump on the bandwagon." I have been able to direct millions of investor dollars because I have trained myself to see and understand cutting-edge companies. Here are a few simple questions to help you find out if your prospective industry is on the cutting edge.

1. **How isolated is your market?**

2. **Are there any $100,000,000 companies in or looking at your industry now? Have they left open any holes that you can fill?**

3. **What current events have impacted your market?**

4. **What are the industry growth trends and statistics?**

5. **What percentage of the market can you easily obtain?**

6. **Does your product offer future possibilities for sales? For example, is your product a razor or a razor and a razor blade? Razor companies practically give away the razors because they want you to keep coming back to buy razor blades.**

If the answers to these questions show an industry that is moving the herd, then it's a market with potential.

Forming the Company*

* If your business is already formed, please look over this section because there are many valuable lessons here.

There are many things for you to consider when deciding how you are going to form your company. *First of all, where do you see your company going? Do you see yourself becoming a public company or staying private? This*

should be decided early because it will dictate how you go forward.

Why stay private? Here are a few good reasons. You have control over your company (as long as you have 51% of the stock or are a DBA company). You do not answer to anyone but yourself. It is less expensive and less time consuming to do your business financials and tax returns. You do not have to disclose material events to the public. Competitors do not have access to information about your company that you choose to withhold from the public.

Why go public? One of the main reasons is that companies historically are valued higher when public. Let me explain how valuation works. For example, let's say a company has issued 10,000,000 shares and they earned $1,000,000. That equates to an EPS (earnings per share) of $0.10 (shares issued divided by earnings). Let's say they are in their third year of business and still expect rapid growth. As a private company, the value of that company (depending on industry and market conditions) could be about $2 - 4 million or $0.20 - $0.40 per share. If that same company were to become public (depending on industry and market conditions), it could be valued at 15-30 times earnings, or $1.50 - 3.00 per share.

Other important factors in deciding to go public: it is easier to attract investors and investment capital into your company, and it gives your company a currency (stock) to acquire other companies. Going public also allows you to attract personnel with stock options and lets you cash out some of your interest in your company and possibly still maintain control.

If you are going to stay private, you can choose from many options to structure your company, which I will cover a few of the more common ways.

Company Type	Private Method	Public Method	Berman Differential Added Value*
Annual Earnings	$1,000,000	$1,000,000	
Shares issued	10,000,000	10,000,000	
Earnings per share	$ .10	$ .10	
Company Share Valuation	$0.20-$0.40	$1.30-$3.00	$1.10 - $2.60*
Valuation of Issued Shares	$2 mil to $4 mil	$15 mil - $30 mil	$13 mil - $26 mil*

* The Berman Differential Added Value is the potential Dollar-Value-Difference of doing business one-way over another

First is a DBA (fictitious name statement)

Both a corporation and an individual can do business using a DBA. Sometimes a corporation or individual may want to transact business under a different name than its corporate name or personal name. This is referred to as using an assumed name or assumed corporate name. Some states refer to it as a fictitious name or trade name (not trademark). Some simply call it a DBA or "doing business as," e.g., ABC Corp. doing business as "Mikey's Tires," or Mike Smith doing business as "Mikey's Tires." Using an assumed name allows you to present yourself to the public as different entities.

A **DBA** is very inexpensive to set up (usually around $100); however, it does not offer the protection of a properly-structured corporation. You can be held personally responsible for any business debts if the business doesn't go as planned.

Second is a Partnership

A partnership is a contract between two or more people in a joint business who agree to pool their funds and talent and share in the profits and losses of an enterprise. General partners are responsible for the day-to-day management of partnership activities, whose individual acts are binding on the other partners, and who are personally liable for the partnership's total liabilities. Limited partners contribute only money and are not involved in management decisions; their liability is limited to their investment.

Next is an LLC (Limited Liability Corporation)

A Limited Liability Corporation, or LLC, is frequently referred to as a hybrid between a corporation and a partnership. That is, it is similar to a corporation because it allows for protection from personal liability. Simultaneously, an LLC is comparable to a partnership because it has similar tax advantages. LLC formation is available in all 50 states.

An LLC is what I prefer to set up for businesses if I do not intend on that business becoming a public company. This not only gives you the protection of a corporation, it also allows potential added personal tax benefits if your business loses money in the startup phase.

Lastly, a Corporation

The corporation is a separate and distinct legal entity apart from the owners of the business. A corporation can own property, enter into contracts, and conduct business under its own name.

Corporations afford some personal protection and cost between $200 - 450 to set up. Some states, like California, charge corporations a tax of $820 a year, even if the corporation does not make a profit. Some states may require you to file a state tax return. You should check if your state has such a tax rule before deciding how to structure your company. A DBA may not have an annual tax in your state.

For those who want to chase the public money**, *going public can be more obtainable than you think.*** At 36 years old, I did not know how to take a company public until I participated in taking one public. Later in this book I will talk about the ins-and-outs of going public. Basically, there are two common ways of going public. The first is the prestigious way: **IPO (Initial Public Offering)**. I call this way the white collar way to go public; and the second, more common way, is the **merger** or **reverse merger**, which I refer to as the blue color way to go public.

Now, if your ultimate goal is to become a public company, my choice would be to first structure the company as a corporation. To start out as a DBA and later convert to a corporation could be time consuming, and also costly. In business there are **windows of opportunity** that come and go. I always like to be prepared, so that I have the option to take advantage of them. For instance, in the mid-90s, restaurant IPOs were in high demand for about 24 months. I worked with a client who was poised to take advantage of the market while it was hot. Because they were prepared, they struck while the iron was hot and their IPO was successful. Then, all of a sudden a major restaurant company started to post losses and restaurants were losing their favor in public markets. Had my client not had the option to get in at the right time, his IPO would not have been successful.

Capital Structure/Issuing Shares

When it comes time to issue shares, my clients wonder what type of shares to issue, how many shares to authorize, and how many to issue.

Authorized Shares

Authorized shares are the maximum number of shares, of any class, a company may legally create under the terms of its Articles of Incorporation, a document filed with the Secretary of State where the company is incorporated by the corporation's founders, describing the purpose, place of business, and other details of the corporation. Normally, a corporation provides for future increases in authorized stock by vote of the shareholders. The corporation is not required to issue all the shares authorized and may initially keep issued shares at a minimum to hold down taxes and expenses.

Issued Shares

Issued Shares of a corporation are authorized in the corporate charter and have been issued and are outstanding. These shares represent capital invested by the firm's shareholders and owners, and may be all or only a portion of the number of shares authorized.

Common Shares

Common Shares are units of ownership of a public corporation. Owners typically are entitled to vote on the selection of directors and other important matters, as well as to receive dividends on their holdings.

Preferred Shares

Preferred Shares pay dividends at a specified rate that has preference over common stock in the payment of dividends and the liquidation of assets. Preferred stock does not ordinarily carry voting rights.

Here we go back to private vs. public. I tend to issue all a company's stock to the founders of the company if it is going to stay private and use a different formula for public. For private, I issue 1,000 shares of common stock to the founders. For public, I like to authorize 100,000,000 shares of common stock and 20,000,000 shares of preferred stock. Initially, I issue 5,000,000 - 10,000,000 common shares to the founders. Why? First off, once you are public, stock splits are very expensive and require shareholder notification and voting. If you authorize 100,000,000 shares, your company could grow to a point where you have issued all your stock and your stock goes to $10 per share. At that time, you are a billion dollar company. Get the point? One hundred million shares are enough to carry you for a long time. Why issue 5,000,000 - 10,000,000 shares to the founders in the beginning? You have to start somewhere, and you want to end up with the company's market cap being at least $50,000,000 and the stock in the $3 - 10 range. That gives you the option to issue 1,000,000 - 10,000,000 shares to raise money, bring in management, etc. It also eliminates the excess time and expense to split the stock prior to going public.

Necessity of Audited Financials

If you intend to be public, you are required to have your financials audited, not just prepared, for at least the last two years, preferably from inception of the business, by an SEC-approved accounting firm. This is expensive, for not only the actual audit, but also the disruption in business an audit can cause.

If you remain private, you can use a local bookkeeper or a business accounting system available at any computer store. Remember, you get what you pay for, so good accounting advice could save you a lot in the long run.

Opening the Company

Your first office

Even if you work out of your house, you need to give the illusion that you have an actual corporate office. Here are a few ways to get the most bang for your buck.

Office in your house

You do not want to use your home address for a variety of

reasons. There are mail service companies that rent mailboxes for a monthly fee, around $20 per month. This will usually give you an address like, 123 Main Street, #300, XYZ City. The #300 gives the illusion of an office. Get dedicated phone lines in your house that will not get accidentally picked up by anyone, or when you're talking, people will not hear your dogs barking. I do not like to use an answering machine. If voicemail isn't available to you, have your phones answered by a live answering service.

Executive suites

Executive suite companies rent small offices and usually include services like phone reception, conference rooms, clerical help, copiers, technical support, and other business machines. Generally, these suites are located in professional areas, such as office parks, so when someone either calls or comes in for a meeting, your business presence is professional and legitimate. Some executive suite companies offer the above services even if you don't rent an office space. They answer your phone, collect your mail, allow you to use their conference rooms. The bonus is that you cut costs by not actually paying for a workspace.

Your first facility

How much space do you need? There are two major factors here: have room to expand but do not get buried in a lease or a space too large. What I prefer to do is to "hedge my bets." I usually rent a space I anticipate is large enough to expand into over a three-year period and for the space I do not use, arrange for a sublease (hopefully prior to executing a lease). Now, you have essentially become an executive suite company. You let people use a portion of your space at a premium, which helps offset some of your lease costs. Typically, the smaller the space, the higher the costs are per square foot.

Owning your own building

Once your business is established, you will find it very common for the owners of a successful business to purchase a building. Based on your location, property costs, and interest rates, owning your own building may be beneficial. Here is a good rule of thumb if you are thinking of buying an office location: If you can get a loan for 90% of the cost of the building and the debt service, and building expenses are close to the amount you were paying in rent, you should buy a building. The company pays you rent, you pay the mortgage and other expenses, and you personally gain any appreciation of the property value, as well as any depreciation tax benefits.

Purchasing your office equipment

I can't think of any major business outlay that historically loses 75% of its value the day it is installed, other than furniture. Buying used office furniture is a must. Besides, perfectly new furniture screams "startup." Used furniture gives the illusion you have been in business longer than you have.

Computers, copiers, and fax machines are another story. Manufacturers frequently upgrade their products. I recommend buying a major brand off-the-shelf or through the Internet. Phone systems are a different story. They don't change and get upgraded like computers, but devalue like office furniture. A good used phone system bought from a reputable dealer can usually be bought with a warranty, which parallels your lease, at a fraction of the cost of a new system.

Creating Your Image

Stationary and Logos

You can spend a lot of money and time looking for the right

stationery. I typically collect business cards and letters from people, and when I see one I like, I keep it to copy the next time I start a business. I take the stationery I like to a printer and have my own letterhead and cards made, using the same font, paper, and look. Call any large firm in your industry and ask them to send you information on their product, and use it as a template.

The Corporate Package

Sometimes the first piece of information a potential client, potential investor, or strategic partner receives on your company is your corporate package or brochure. The number-one rule for putting corporate packages together is that they look and feel complete and have a careful balance between being thorough, but not packed with useless information.

If you don't have a corporate logo or design, start out with an easy cost-effective winner. Buy white glossy folders. Almost any color you decide to print on it will look good, and, of course, match. Now, what information should be put in the corporate packet?

1. **Letter from the CEO or founder**

2. **Management biographies**

3. **Information on your product or service**

4. **Industry research**

5. **Strategic alliances and corporate partners**

This is just an idea on how to get started. If your package seems to be missing something, search for articles about your industry (the Internet is a great source) and fill space in your package with it. When all else fails, call one of your competitors and look at their information for ideas.

PART THREE
{ Business Development 101 }

Ever make a decision that cost you a lot of money? When you did, I bet the first thing you told yourself is that you will never do that again. Well, I have made decisions that have both cost me millions of dollars and made me millions of dollars.

This section is packed full of my hard-earned knowledge regarding various strategies that show you how to grow your business, increase profits, minimize losses, and most importantly, keep more money. It's a must-read section for everyone from beginners to billionaires.

Banking and Finance

Basic business banking has historically stayed consistent and unchanged. The age-old adage that **"a bank doesn't want to loan money to you if you need it"** is still true. So what do you do when you want to borrow money when you need it? Well, that's where careful planning and relationship building comes in handy.

What do banks want?

They want deposits and your daily bank balances to stay as high as possible and to make risk-free loans!

Okay, here is where people make some basic mistakes. The first one is, don't cash any checks. Have you ever applied for one of those easy-qualifier mortgages? What the lenders base your income on is cash flow. So let's say you deposited three checks for $5,000 every month into the **same bank account** and did that for **three months in a row**. You've given the appearance that you have $15,000 a month in income. Now, if each month you cashed one of those checks for cash, then you would have only deposited $10,000 a month, which gives the appearance you have only $10,000 in income, when in fact you have $15,000. Rule #1 is to deposit all your checks into the same account each month and write checks or transfer money from there.

Referrals

Referrals are a great way to build a relationship with a bank at no cost to you. Refer your employees, friends, and business associates to a bank. This is a key to relationship building. I have referred hundreds of people to my banker. A few of them turned out to grow into some of the bank's biggest accounts. What does that mean to me? The banker wants my referrals and will stretch the limits for me and give me his best terms available for a few referrals. This takes little time and everybody wins.

Build your credit

When you first start banking at a new bank, apply for a small loan that you don't need. Get to know the bank officers and build a relationship. They love to make loans that people don't need. Pay it off early. Not in the first three months, but any time after that is OK. Next, go get another loan, a little larger, and do the same thing. Eventually, when you need a loan, your track record will help substantially.

Pick the right bank

Are you a small fish in a big pond? I like to study banks' advertising and brochures and see what their specialty is or what type of client they want to service. One bank may specialize in real estate second trustees, another in auto loans, and yet another in small business loans. I prefer banks with anywhere from 3-10 branches. Single-branch banks tend to have a limited scope of loans they will do; multi-branch banks think more on the entrepreneurial side of growth. When you start out building banking relationships, remember that you not only build it with the bank, but with the bank officer too. The banker I started out with 30 years ago is still my main banker today. He has switched banks around five times as he grew in the banking business. He takes with him a memory of the accounts I have referred to him and our relationship everywhere he goes. He has written me reference letters for other purposes, which I have used to grow my businesses.

Pushing the envelope

What if you have enough savings but the loan you want requires more monthly income than you have?

I know what some people do in order to get a larger, no-income verified, easy qualifier mortgage than for which they qualify. They use a two-bank system to get the job done. Here is what they do. Let's say their income is $6,000 a month and they would need cash flow of $7,500 a month to qualify for the loan they want. First, they deposit their savings into an account in one bank (Bank A), then each month they withdraw $1,500 from Bank A and deposit in to a different bank (Bank B). Now each month they also deposit $6,000 in income into Bank B. When someone looks at their last three bank statements at Bank B, they now show $7,500 a month in deposits. This was for example only. ***Depending on the loan application, paperwork, and the disclosures you make to the lender, this could be illegal. I would review this with a qualified lawyer in your state before doing anything like this.***

What if I have bad credit or no credit?

"Abominable credit"—that's what my first banker said about my credit report. A few years later he lent me $1,000,000. My banker liked me because I treated him with respect and always acted professionally when I was in his bank. I did what I outlined in the previous paragraphs and it worked. If you have bad credit, you need to work on repairing it. Now, there are plenty credit repairing agencies out there and you're free to hire them. I hired a few, and what I learned from my experience was they basically got a copy of my credit report, wrote a letter disputing every delinquent account, and mailed it to the credit bureaus. I affectionately call these "bad credit blow-off letters." Apparently the credit-reporting agency must then send a letter to all the creditors and ask them to verify the debt and unless the party reporting the bad credit verifies the bad mark within 30 days, the mark must come off. Now, I continued to do the same process every three months and after about a year my credit was better.

What is a credit score?

Credit Bureau scores are often called "FICO scores," being that most credit bureau scores in the United States are produced from software developed by Fair Isaac and Company (FICO). FICO scores are provided to lenders by the major credit reporting agencies. Credit scores provide a guide to future risk based solely on credit report data. The higher the score, the lower the indicated risk. But a score does not indicate whether a specific individual will be a "good" or "bad" customer.

While many lenders use credit scores to help them make lending decisions, each lender has its own strategy, including the level of risk it finds acceptable for a given credit product. There is no single "cutoff score" used by all lenders and there are many additional factors that lenders use to determine your actual interest rates.

It is important to note that credit scoring is NOT underwriting a loan application; it is one variable that is looked at in underwriting a loan application.

How credit scoring works

Credit scoring is calculated by a mathematical equation that evaluates many types of information that are in a consumer's credit file at that specific repository/bureau. By comparing this information to the patterns in hundreds of thousands of past credit reports, the score identifies the lender's level of future credit risk. In order for a credit score to be calculated on a consumer's credit file, the file must contain at least one account, which has been open for six months or longer. In addition, the file must contain at least one account that has been updated in the past six months. This ensures that there is enough information—and enough recent information—in the credit file on which to base a score.

What a credit score considers

Listed below are the five main categories of information that credit scores evaluate, along with their approximate level of importance.

1. **Payment history—35% of the score's weight**

2. **Amounts owed—30% of the score's weight**

3. **Length of credit history—15% of the score's weight**

4. **New credit inquiries—10% of the score's weight**

5.**Types of credit used—10% of the score's weight**

What a credit score ignores

Credit scores consider a wide range of information on the consumer's credit report. However, they do not consider a consumer's race, color, religion, national origin, sex, and marital status. U.S. law prohibits considering these facts when scoring credit, as well as any receipt of public assistance, or the exercise of any consumer right under the Consumer Credit Protection Act (CCPA.)

SBA Loans

The Small Business Administration (SBA) is an independent agency of the federal government, established by Congress, to advise and help finance the nation's small businesses. The agency also works with thousands of lending, educational, and training institutions nationwide.

The SBA enables its lending partners to provide financing to small businesses when funding is otherwise unavailable on reasonable terms by guaranteeing major portions of loans made to small businesses. Even if your local bank has turned you down, a SBA lender may be able to help you. ***Many SBA*** *lenders will give special consideration to minority and/or women-owned businesses. You will still need to meet the credit criteria. These are loans, not grants.* However, the eligibility requirements and credit criteria of SBA programs are very broad in order to accommodate a wide range of financing needs.

When a small business applies to a lending partner for a loan, the lender reviews the application and decides if it merits a loan on its own or if it requires additional support in the form of an SBA guaranty. The lender then requests SBA backing on the loan. In guaranteeing the loan, the SBA assures the lender that in the event the borrower does not repay the loan, the government will reimburse the lending partner for a portion of its loss. By providing this guaranty, the SBA is able to help tens of thousands of small businesses every year get financing they would not otherwise obtain.

To qualify for an SBA guaranty, a small business must meet the SBA's criteria, and the lender must certify that it could not provide funding on reasonable terms without an SBA guaranty. The SBA can guarantee as much as 85% on loans of up to $150,000 and 75% on loans of more than $150,000. In most cases, the maximum guaranty is $1,000,000. There are higher loan limits for international trade, defense-dependent small firms affected by defense reductions, and certified development company loans.

Establishing a Merchant Account

Being able to accept credit cards is easy as 1, 2, 3

Wrong. Setting up a merchant account can be very difficult, especially if you are a mail order or Internet-based business. With the ever-increasing problem of credit card fraud, banks are making it tougher to obtain merchant accounts (the ability to accept credit cards). Banks are mainly interested in the following when considering establishing a merchant account.

1. **Credit history and financial strength of the business principal.**

2. **What is the product you are selling?**

3. **How are you advertising your product?**

4. **What is your return policy?**

5. **How you accept payment?**

Credit History and financial strength

If you have personal credit problems, the bank will likely consider you to be too risky to receive a merchant account. If you have bad credit, you should look for a partner or someone else with whom you have a close relationship to be the principal on the merchant account application.

What is the product you are selling?

Why would a bank care about your product? Because they don't want a high percentage of returns, cancellations, or fraud. If you are selling a vitamin that makes you lose 50 pounds while you sleep, and you guarantee that feature, a bank will be skeptical about your product and will probably decline your request.

How are you advertising your product?

If you make outlandish claims that your product will do things that we all know aren't possible or guarantee results that are overzealous, you will make your application more difficult to consider. Banks do not like to see guarantees like "lose weight while you're sleeping" or "double your money back."

What is your return policy?

Banks lose money when they pay for a staff to talk to unhappy consumers. If you are not willing to give dissatisfied customers their money back, you are going to eat into the bank's profits, so in most cases you must offer a money-back policy to use a merchant account.

I don't know where to get a merchant account.

No problem. Go to our website at www.BruceABerman.com, and you will find a link to a merchant account company that specializes in setting up merchant accounts for startup businesses.

This company provides affordable electronic payment solutions to help new and existing businesses increase their bottom-line profitability. They also specialize in assisting all types of businesses (retail, internet, mail order, phone order, home-based) with the following "value-added" services and merchant benefits:

Value-Added Service	Merchant Benefits
Credit & Debit Card Processing	• increase sales by providing more forms of payments to your customers • save money with low processing rates and affordable terminal options • maximize cash flow with 24-48 hour electronic depositing • receive 24-hour toll-free customer support

Value-Added Service (cont.)	**Merchant Benefits** (cont.)
Electronic Check Processing & Guarantee	• receive 100% guaranteed payment on all bounced checks • eliminate bank non-sufficient funds and collection fees • 24-hour electronic depositing eliminates 5-10 day float time with paper checks • eliminate time-wasting trips to the bank to deposit daily checks • increase sales revenues and profits
Gift & Loyalty Card Processing	• increase customer traffic and purchases • increase customer loyalty and brand awareness • maximize business exposure

To receive information on establishing a merchant account, go to our website (www.BruceABerman.com)

Contract Negotiating

Do you look like, act like, and exude the aura of a successful businessperson? *Everyone wants to do business with a winner.* Business owners who come to me for personal help give me up to a 10% equity position in their company for my consulting services. Now most of these business owners believe that their companies have the potential to become $100,000,000 companies. What do I do? I tell them my fee is 10%. When I reveal my fee, I can feel the business owner's mind churning. The first question they ask themselves is, "Is this guy worth $10,000,000 and is this what he charges everyone?" I tell them right up front that I only take on clients I think can make me several million dollars, and that I turn down prospective clients all the time because I don't believe they are going to make it.

Why do they give me such a high fee?

1. **They need my services.**

2. **I have a great corporate image package (taught in this book).**

3. **They know, upfront, that I am not some guy trying to make my first million dollar score. It's more like business as usual.**

4. **Remember, I started out poor, so I had to originally create the illusion, by the way I look, act, dress, and carry myself, that I am someone who already has millions of dollars. You don't get what you deserve, you get what you negotiate.**

Remember, don't try to negotiate business transactions before you have followed the plan laid out in this book and have finished creating your Illusion.

Personal Appearance

First and foremost, if you do not have any physical limitations that prevent you from staying in good physical condition, get in shape. If you can not mange your own physical appearance, how can you manage a business? I personally like to work out before an important meeting. It gives me an edge. I usually am very alert after a workout and on top of my game.

Dress for the occasion. First impressions are vital in business. *There is no second chance for a first impression.* If you are in an industry that requires a suit and tie, wear one. You should have one suit of higher quality than your daily work suits. Wear your best suit to important meetings. Make sure it is always freshly dry-cleaned and pressed. I usually leave one complete change of clothes at my office for any unexpected business situations. Most importantly, your suit needs to fit. If you have gained or lost weight recently, have it tailored or get a new suit. I like to buy a new tie for special business meetings; I feel it gives me an "edge." Ties, belts, and shoes tell a lot about a person's character. If you go out and buy an expensive suit but wear cheap shoes or belt, it is a dead giveaway you're not a savvy businessperson.

If your industry calls for different attire, just use the ground rules of looking your best and purchasing one new item that gives you the mental edge. Have you seen the Viagra commercial where a man walks through an office and everyone asks him if he got a new suit, haircut, had been working out, got a raise, or just got back from vacation? Instead of these things, he had confidence because he had started taking Viagra. This same confidence can come across by the way you appear.

Be prepared

Practice your presentation and know the facts. Go to the most negative person you know and ask him to critique your pitch, holding nothing back.

Keep your presentation simple. One of the biggest mistakes business owners make is talking down to people, because the business owner knows more about the business than the person on the other side of the table. If the other person knew more about your business than you, they wouldn't be there. I have seen more educated people fail because they refuse to talk in layman's terms.

Do not ask questions to which you don't already know the answer. If you put together a proposal for 1,000 units of a product, and you ask the company how many they need and they say 100,000 units, you are not prepared.

Qualify the parties

Know with whom you are dealing. Why are they meeting with you? What do they want? So many times I have walked into meetings and everyone involved has a different agenda. For example, I recently attended a meeting where my firm was going to provide investor relations services for a prospective company. The first thing I did, once everyone involved was there, was hand out my business cards and ask for theirs. There was one person with a card without a title listed, which gave me no clue as to why he was there. I politely asked about his position with the company. By reviewing the cards, I got a good feeling about who wanted my services and who didn't.

It was apparent to me that they had an internal investor relations (IR) department with four staff members that probably cost them $10,000 - $15,000 a month to operate. Our contract was going to be for $4,500 a month to outsource the IR. The person whose card did not have a title was the person in charge of the internal IR program. In other words, he was going to get laid off or transferred as a cost- saving measure when the company hired me.

As I made my proposal, the IR person kept throwing out unreasonable questions. Since I had pre-qualified him and knew his motivations, I was able to handle him correctly. I let him ask three questions that were obviously meant to derail my presentation, then I looked at the CEO and asked him if it would be OK to save the questions for the end because my presentation would probably answer most of the questions being asked. In that way, we would save time, especially since there were eight people in the room. The CEO smiled, thought about the $10,000 a month I would save them, and agreed. Needless to say, I walked away with a contract.

ABC, Always Be Closing

This is an old cliché but it is true today. I don't know if you have ever seen the movie *Glengarry Glen Ross*. If you haven't seen it, rent it. The events in the movie provide a strong example of sales-closing techniques.

What does it mean to always be closing? It means you repeatedly ask for the order. I have added to that cliché, **Continually Remove Objections While Selling, CROWS.**

Here is an example of using ABC and CROWS. You are selling a copy machine to Mr. Jones. Mr. Jones wants to purchase a copier that prints 100 copies a minute, has a document feeder, collator, and can be purchased for $7,500. You can sell him a machine like that for $7,500; however, you earn a bonus if you sell it to him for $8,000.

Now, if you have followed my previous suggestions in this book, you appear to Mr. Jones as the top representative in your company. You have an air of confidence, one that exudes success and product knowledge. You know your product line inside and out, and have a basic sales plan ready to go. Mr. Jones is walking out of your office today with a new copy machine he so desperately needs. You have already asked Mr. Jones the basic qualifying questions and know he has the authority, need, and money to purchase a machine today for his company. You are a winner, and a winner never quits and a quitter never wins.

1. Mr. Jones, if this copy machine could print 100 copies a minute, would you buy it? **Here you are asking a closing question, "Would you buy it?" ABC (Here it is ok to ask a question which the answer can be no because it sets them up for a closing question next.)**

2. Mr. Jones, how many copies per minute do you need your copier to copy? **Mr. Jones answered no to the previous**

question, so you came back with another closing
question and objection removal. ABC and CROWS.

3. OK Mr. Jones, this copier does meet your 100 copies per
   minute need, but you're right, it doesn't have a collator. If I
   can add a collator to this machine, would it then meet your
   needs? **You have now removed the objection on copies
   per minute. Don't ever go back once you have removed
   an objection, put it in your pocket, you will need it
   later. By saying, "If I can add a collator," you are
   getting him to make a partial commitment and you
   haven't committed to anything yet. Turning, "if I can"
   into "yes I can" is a bargaining chip for you to keep in
   your pocket. This is an example of ABC and CROWS.**

4. Mr. Jones, we are making progress, however, you're right, this
   copier doesn't have a document feeder, but I may be able to
   add one now. If I could add one, would you purchase the
   copier? **"Making progress" is telling him both of you
   have agreed to all previously discussed objections.
   Again, ABC and CROWS.**

5. Mr. Jones, what do I need to add to this copier for you to
   purchase it? **This is when you are actually asking for the
   order for the first time. You have removed his previous
   objections and the only thing left is price. ABC and
   CROWS.**

6. As you know, Mr. Jones, by our pricing, with all your
   requested options, the price of this copier, the way you want
   it is $10,000. How soon do you need it delivered? **That is a
   great closing statement. You aren't saying buy it now,
   but you are asking him to agree now to purchase it at
   $10,000. If he says he doesn't want to pay $10,000,
   you follow up with if we can agree on a price, how soon
   would you want it delivered? ABC and CROWS.**

7. That we can do for you Mr. Jones. We can deliver this copier to you tomorrow. Now, I understand you don't want to pay $10,000. How much do you want to pay? **Here you have agreed to sell the machine and he has agreed to buy it, so we are down to one thing, price. ABC and CROWS.**

8. Mr. Jones, $5,000 is not a very reasonable offer for this copy machine but if I could get it for you at $7,500, would you buy it? **The lowest you can go is $7,500 and that is the most he wants to pay. Here you are going to ask him to commit to a price but you haven't agreed to one yet. ABC and CROWS.**

9. Good news, Mr. Jones, my boss has allowed me to knock off $1,500 and I can sell you this machine exactly how you want it for $8,500. That is a 15% reduction from list price and a great deal. All I need is your signature here. **Remember you had no sales today before Mr. Jones walked into your store. If you don't ask for the order, you are not going to get it, and you still have more cards to play.**

10. Mr. Jones, I know you only want to pay $7,500 and $7,500 is a reasonable offer, but I can't sell you the machine for $7,500. However, tomorrow is the end of our sales quarter, and I am two machines shy of making bonus and I really want to make bonus this quarter, because it is a four-day trip for my wife and me. (Sigh and seem a little disappointed when you say what is coming up.) I wouldn't normally do this, but I will cut my commission, which is approximately $550, to close this sale today. That means you can buy this machine for $7,950, which is more than $2,000 under list price, and a steal for a piece of equipment that is exactly what you're looking for and have it delivered tomorrow. (this tactic does work because the customer believes they are getting a price reduction at your expense)

Okay, at $7,950 you are still going to get your bonus (minus $50.) He feels you, the salesman, aren't getting rich off him, and at this point, 90% of the legitimate people would buy. If Mr. Jones asks you where your trip is, it needs to be something not too extravagant, because he doesn't want to think he is sending you to Europe. ABC and CROWS.

11. Mr. Jones, I just went back and told my boss where we were and when he saw I was willing to give up my commission to make bonus, he authorized me to go ahead and sell you the machine at your price of $7,500. I have never seen him do that before, but I think he wants to keep everyone happy. My guess is, he has a quota too, but I am not sure. **Only if you have to use the last card, and really give up your bonus, do you do this. ABC and CROWS.**

Objection Removal

Removing objections is one of the most valuable tools a businessperson can develop. It is not only an effective business tool but it works in your personal life too. People, in general, throw out unwarranted objections instead of admitting that they aren't qualified or cannot afford a product. So, by developing the skill of removing objections, you can be more productive by spending time with people who really are qualified and interested, rather than out for a Sunday drive.

My son was supposed to set up a meeting at a college to go over his high school transcripts and see what classes he needed to take next semester to be eligible for a certain college. We had a photocopy of his transcripts to bring with us. I asked him if he set up the meeting at the college yet, and he said no. He threw out the objection that the college needed the official transcripts showing which classes were college prep courses vs. electives. He was throwing out an objection. He is 17 and many teens his age do the same thing. I realized that it would take weeks to get official transcripts and he needed to have them now. I removed his objection by telling him to mark on the transcripts which were college prep and which were electives, take that to the college counselor, and inform them that an official version would be coming. Hence, there was no need to wait.

If I Can

I love those words. "If I can do this, will you buy?" "If I can do this, will you work for us?" "If I can do this, are you in a position to enter that agreement?" By saying, "if I can," you are basically getting someone to counter his own offer. You offer me $16,000 for a car that has a sticker price of $19,000. I come back and say, "let me talk to my boss, but if I can get you the car for $17,000, would you buy it?" You say yes. You have just come up $1,000 and I haven't even countered yet. I come back and say, "OK, you said you were willing to pay $17,000; we are at $18,000, let us meet halfway at $17,500 and we are done." This happens every day that way with car dealers, although, there are usually several rounds of going back and forth. The next time you buy a car, watch for, "if I can."

Legal Strategies

Litigation is a part of business: get used to it

The age-old adage that the only ones who make money in a lawsuit are the attorneys is true for the naive and the uninformed. Don't get me wrong, I hate spending money on legal fees, but they are a necessary evil. The trick is to keep them to a minimum and be successful. I have, on occasion, walked out of a courtroom and felt like the legal fees I spent made me money.

Where did I get my legal degree?

Some people go to college, then law school to get their legal degrees. I don't know what a legal education costs these days but it is safe to say anywhere from $50,000 to $500,000. I got mine the old fashioned way, by earning it. If I add up all the fees and litigation costs I have paid and that of the companies I owned or ran, the legal fees would be several million dollars. You can't get the legal education I have in school. When you actually have millions of your own dollars on the line and are paying fees, you learn and feel things that can't be taught. My business experience in the law encompasses the following areas:

1. **Contractual agreements and disputes**

2. **Collections**

3. **Private placement memorandums**

4. **Writ of attachments, judgments and liens**

5. **Internal Revenue disputes**

6. **Partnership agreements and corporate structure**

7. **National and international contracts and financings**

8. **Bankruptcies; Chapters 7, 11, and 13**

9. **Employee, employer, and labor board**

10. **Legal opinions and securities laws**

11. **Real estate law**

12. **Depositions, discovery, and document production**

13. **Mediation, disclosure, and compliance**

14. **Settlement agreements and negotiations**

15. **Reducing legal costs and fees**

Cover Your Ass

You can never be too careful in business, especially when you're raising money from investors. I always have a CYA (cover your ass) file for support documentation. Whenever you make a business statement, quote, or disclaimer, keep files of all your supportive documents in a place you can refer to later if needed.

Have you ever read an offering document? They are full of disclosures that explain all the ways you can lose money. Some uninformed people believe that the reason disclosures are there is because management doesn't think they are going to be successful; therefore, the company has bad management. Not the case. Someone who covers his or her ass with disclosures is a very wise businessperson, the more disclosures the merrier.

Stay out of court

The lesson that I learned is to stay out of court and settle every dispute you can. Unlike filing a personal injury lawsuit, where the attorneys work on a contingency basis, in most, if not all cases, business litigation tends to be made on an hourly fee.

The client is the enemy

I read a book once called *Shark Tank*. It was written about a law firm that represented my company. The firm was called Finley Kumble. They were a prestigious law firm with several hundred lawyers in several high profile locations. When I went to their office in Los Angeles, they had two floors of a major high-rise building with an opulent private staircase between the two floors.

The firm went out of business and was later garnered the nickname of "Finally Crumbled." Why they went out of business was a humorous story itself but not germane to this book. In the book, *Shark Tank*, the firm looked at its clients as the "enemy," instead of people to whom to give the benefit of the doubt, and who are always right; they looked at us, the clients, as the enemy! They wanted our money and lots of it. Bill, bill, bill was their philosophy.

Not all firms are like "Finally Crumbled," but it is important to look at their example of where we, the clients, potentially stand as a lawyer's client. There are all sorts of law firms, from the sole practitioner to the 1,000-person international firm. A big law firm's favorite strategy is to have you meet with the more senior partner in the firm, who bills the higher rate, and he usually has an impressive list of qualifications. Now, is he going to do the work on your case? No. A junior lawyer will do most of the work. Big law firms work junior lawyers to death and the senior partners review their work and bill almost all of the fees at the senior partner rate.

One time I was telling a friend of mine that I was paying a fortune in legal fees. He asked me who my lawyer was and when I told him, he said he had a friend using the same lawyer with the same complaint. I got together with his friend and we compared our bills for two of the same months. We found that there were 26 hours billed on some days and 30 on others. The same attorney had billed us both on the same day, on several occasions, for more than 24 hours of work.

We jointly approached the attorney, listened to his explanation (it was good; I only hire good attorneys), and he reduced both our bills substantially. We didn't have to bring up the obvious (we could have him disbarred) because it would do no good. He knew and we knew that he knew we knew.

How do I keep my legal bills reasonable?

Don't hire an attorney. That's not the answer. First things first, understand who you are hiring. You don't always need a large firm. Many people make the mistake by thinking that if they hire the biggest and the best-known law firm they can't lose, kind of like the bully syndrome. Did you ever see *Raiders of the Lost Ark*? There was a scene where a sword-wielding warrior threatened Harrison Ford with a series of amazing hand movements and swords. It looked like Ford was doomed. Then he reached in his pocket and pulled out a pistol and shot the big warrior dead. Don't be fooled into having a big warrior.

There are times to use big firms and there are times to use small ones. I personally like being the big fish in a small pond and go for the small firms in matters I believe are going to actually go to litigation. I use big firms when I am doing an offering document. I usually get a fixed price up front and know what the cost will be. Investors like seeing a big firm's name on offering documents, and I like the feeling of having the big firm sign off on my security offering, so that if they make a mistake, they will be there to protect their name and reputation (except "Finally Crumbled") and, ultimately, my behind.

Okay, you hired the big firm. Now what?

The first and second bill set the tone for the relationship. Don't be afraid and intimated by the big firm. When you get your first bill, go over it, line-by-line. See who is doing the hourly work. It is usually itemized. I had one firm bill me for conversations with a junior partner of whom I had never heard, let alone spoken with on any occasion. You will usually see the juniors doing a great deal of work. Get to know the junior lawyers, speak to them once a week, monitor what they are doing, and keep accurate notes. When you get the bill, you can say, "Hey, I talked to Bob every Friday, and he gave the impression that he worked five hours each week but my bill is about 15 hours each week." Get the drift? Be politically correct, don't paint someone into a box, but monitor their progress. I have cut my legal fees with big firms by almost half on most cases.

Do the lawyers need to bring three people to a deposition? Not in most cases. Find out before a deposition who the law firm is sending and why. It is a common practice for large law firms to send one or two junior lawyers to a deposition for the purpose of training them and billing you more. Hence, you pay to train someone of little-known value to you. Believe it or not, the senior partners don't like to go to depositions because it is not cost effective to them. When they are out of the office, they can only bill so many hours in a day. When they're in the office, their practice of rounding out billing increments puts a lot more available billing hours in the day.

Big firms win cases in a variety of ways. One of the most common ways goes something like this: the senior partner tells you that your opponent in the case has retained a small firm. The senior partner's big firm is going to bury the opposing firm and client in paperwork, motions, interrogatories, notice of depositions, document productions, notice to produce, etc. He will sic two junior associates on it, and they will create so much turmoil for the opposing law firm and client it will make them want to settle in your favor. Sounds good? Just remember, turnabout is fair play. The small firm will probably take all the document production, notices and interrogatories, etc., you slapped on them, hand them to a paralegal, and ask them to request the same from you.

What have you just done? You created a bunch of legal fees for yourself and the opposing party. Congratulations. You fell into a lawyer's favorite trap. Remember, you, the client, are the enemy.

Now if you were in a dispute over $100,000, you may have just run up $25,000 in legal fees between you and the other party and you just put the possibility of a favorable settlement another $25,000 apart. You have to be in charge and make the decisions on your legal strategy. ***Get the facts from your lawyer and always ask yourself whose best interest is this in, the lawyers or mine? Remember, you make the decisions.***

Having the law and facts on your side means you are going to win the case, doesn't always mean you will win the case. The winner does not have to be the one who is right; it is the one who makes the judge believe he or she is right. Some defendants go to big firms hoping that the large firm will bring them credibility in the judge's or jurors' eyes. It just brings a large firm.

The big tip

One case, in particular, taught me the most valuable tip on legal strategy. I had a dispute with a company, XYZ. They were supposed to deliver 100 products for which we were paying $25,000 each, or $2,500,000 total. We pre-sold the product for $50,000 each, a profit of $2,500,000. The shipment came and the supplier had only shipped 50 of the products. Our purchase contract was for 100 units and had no provision for only 50 to be delivered. Before we paid them for the first 50 ($1,250,000), I started to investigate if they were on schedule to deliver the next 50 products. I found out the reason they only shipped 50 is because they were having problems and could not deliver the quantity they promised.

Company XYZ said they could deliver the product eventually and wanted us to pay for the other 50 and wait for delivery. The problem was that my buyer wouldn't wait. ***During a phone conversation, Company XYZ threatened to sue me*** if we didn't take all 100 when they finally had them done. My mentors always told me ***"don't make threats you don't intend to carry out."*** It wasn't too smart for them to threaten to sue me. Our conversation was on a Friday. I told them to meet me on Monday afternoon at my office to see if we could resolve the issue. I got busy fast. I met with my attorney over the weekend, and prepared a lawsuit against company XYZ. We sued them for the $2,500,000 of profit we should have received, plus $5,000,000 in punitive damages for not delivering the product to me and damaging my reputation. We filed the suit on Monday morning, and I was ready for the Monday afternoon meeting.

Company XYZ came to the meeting, where I had my attorney in attendance. They got nasty and would not bend on allowing me to cancel the 50 units that they were going to be shipping late, saying there was no agreement for me to cancel a late order and would not lend any credence to, "I lost my buyer and my profit on the late orders."

I looked at them and said, "I guess we will just have to go your route and see what happens in court." They got a little heated and said they were going to sue me. I looked at my lawyer and instructed him to serve them with the suit I prepared. Now they were puzzled. "You're suing us?" said the CEO of XYZ Company. "Yes, I am just following your suggestion of resolving this in court," I replied.

My mentor used to tell me, ***"Possession is 9/10 of the law."*** I had in my possession the money I had received from my client for the goods, $2,500,000. The next valuable lesson I had learned was the person that is most right doesn't always win the case. It is the person who convinces the judge they are right who wins. In order to have the most credibility in a lawsuit, ***I always want to be the plaintiff and not the defendant. Being a plaintiff gives you the appearance of the most injured party.***

Now, do you think I wanted this case to go forward fast? No, I didn't. What was my hurry? I had all the money I really wanted, which was the $2,500,000. I just wanted to keep it all. I never expected to receive a penny for punitive damages. It was just a ploy to further my appearance that I was damaged.

Thirty days later I got their answer and cross complaint. They wanted their $1,250,000 for the first 50 units, and they made the mistake of asking for the $1,250,000 for the units they hadn't shipped. Now, do you think they were going to ship those units when they were made? No. So now they look even worse.

They made the mistake of hiring a big firm and trying to bury my small firm in paperwork. All they accomplished was to provide a series of reasons to stall, stall, stall; after all, I already had the $2,500,000 million, so what's my hurry?

We finally went to court. The judge asked if Company XYZ delivered the second 50 units and they replied that they had not supplied the second half of the order. The judge threw out their claim for the second 50 or $1,250,000. By their not delivering the second 50 units, I was able to prove we were damaged and the judge ordered that we receive our $2,500,000 in profit. In order to achieve that, they were not to get paid for the first $1,250,000 and there would be no punitive award because they did not purposely delay the order of the second 50 units. My attorney threw a fit about the punitive damages not being awarded. I could barely keep a straight face. I was so happy with the outcome because we kept the whole $2,500,000, which I used for the last few years. When my attorney walked outside, I looked at him and said, "Why did you make such a big argument on us losing the punitive?" He told me, "I didn't want the judge or the other lawyer to rethink the other $2,500,000, because basically, Bruce, the defendant got nothing and you got $2,500,000." "Thank you." Lesson learned, *always be the plaintiff and possession is 9/10 of the law.*

Look at this situation if I had played it differently. Let's say I paid XYZ the $1,250,000 (possession is 9/10 of the law) for the first 50, then they turned around and sued me (plaintiff vs. defendant) for not taking delivery of the other 50 units. At that point they would have had a great case and $1,250,000 of the cash (which I kept) and I would not have had much of a defense.

Powerful legal strategies

There are a few things I have learned and believe are very basic in litigation. I have already given you three: **try to settle every dispute out of court, possession is 9/10 of the law and be the plaintiff rather than the defendant.**

Now, what do you do when the case starts? Well, it's like poker. How would you like to see the other guy's cards before you bet? Litigation can be that way. **Strike first.**

Usually deposition and discovery notices have a timeframe in which to respond. If you serve the other party first, the clock starts ticking. Now, what usually happens is the opposing side will ask for a continuance and you agree, but make sure you get a stipulation saying they have to respond first—that way you get to see their cards before showing yours.

Philosophy of a Deposition

So they want to take your deposition. In the beginning the deposing lawyer will ask very mundane questions like where do you live, how old are you, spell your name, etc. They are not getting useless information. They are preconditioning you to answer their questions without any reservation on your part.

The most valuable thing I ever heard from an attorney is "a fish doesn't get caught if he doesn't open his mouth."

I have spent a lot of money in legal fees and that's what sticks out as the best single piece of advice. When you're getting your deposition taken, just realize that anything you say that helps your case will not be used by the other attorney. You will never win him over with your charm or any other tactics. This is business. Most law firms have a few lawyers who do nothing but take depositions. Why? Because they are good at it.

I had one attorney show up to a deposition in a Philly's baseball hat. He knew I was born in Philadelphia, and he was trying to bond with me. I looked at him and told him I hate sports (before I was under oath). The pencil banged. Attorneys know when you are thinking and will try to break your attention so that you spout out the answer they want, rather than the one you want. Be aware of their tactics. I was getting into a sensitive area, and I had just returned from a bathroom break so I couldn't ask for another one (when you need a break, have a small bladder). So, I asked the attorney to quit tapping his pen on the desk. He said he wasn't; and I had him. I restated he was tapping it, which was making it hard to concentrate and answer his questions. Then I said, "You don't have to raise your voice at me" (keep in mind this is being recorded in print). Oh, did that make him mad! He went on the record for at least 10 minutes: yadayadayada. I got my break and regrouped.

Some of my favorite deposition responses

1. **I don't recall? (Ever heard that one before?)**

2. **Can I think about it and get back to you later?**

3. **Can you repeat that question?**

4. **Can you repeat it again, I'm still confused?**

5. **I am sorry you don't like my answer.**

6. **I am not sure. Would you like me to guess?**

7. **I didn't hear you. Can you speak up?**

8. **You don't need to raise your voice, I heard you.**

9. **You want me to estimate or approximate? Do you mean guess?**

10. **I am cold. Do you mind if I go to the car and get my sweater?**

11. **It's getting hot in here. Can you adjust the air? I need a break until you do, I feel faint.**

If you want to get out of a deposition once it has started, you can get the judge mad, maybe be sanctioned, and perhaps jeopardize your case; but, if you are convinced the choice of going forward is worse then canceling, below are a few things that shake up depositions.

1. **When you get back from lunch: "I had a drink on an empty stomach and I feel like I can't answer any more questions."**

2. **Take a doctor prescribed Valium or other medicines during a break, come back and tell them you're having trouble.**

3. **"I need to go to the doctor, my blood pressure is dangerously high."**

Tax Strategies

Why work 40 hours a week for someone else when you can work 60 hours a week for yourself?

Granted, there are drawbacks about working for yourself but there are benefits too. Let's look at tax strategies. Here is a semi-hypothetical situation about a guy who owned a palm tree farm and had been a DBA for years. I told him several times over the years to incorporate it for a variety of reasons, but he didn't want to spend the few hundred dollars to do it and wasn't open to listening to me about the benefits of a limited liability corporation. His big argument was that it was a family business and always would be a family business. Well, the palm tree farm did very well. In fact, he opened four more in various locations. Then, he got an unsolicited offer to sell all the palm trees to a major developer for about $4,000,000. He took the offer and sold all the palm trees and after paying income tax he netted just over $2,400,000. He was so proud of himself that I really hated to give him a, "I told you so," but he made the mistake of asking me what I thought. That opened the door for me to explain how he gave the government a million dollars he could have kept.

Liquidity of Company Assets	Selling Inventory	Selling Inventory For Stock	Berman Differential Added Value*
Price Sold	$4,000,000	$4,000,000	
Quantity	Entire Inventory	Entire Inventory	
Tax Paid	$1,600,000	$600,000	
Income Type	Ordinary Income	Capital Gains	$1,000,000*

* The Berman Differential Added Value is the potential Dollar-Value-Difference of doing business one-way over another

You see, he sold his inventory creating $4,000,000 in ordinary income. Now, the business, which is basically gone, has taxable income of $4,000,000. That transaction will be taxed at the highest tax rate, close to 40%, so he will owe taxes of almost $1,600,000 on that transaction and net $2,400,000 after federal tax. Now, if he had incorporated, as I told him to three years earlier, instead of selling the inventory, he would have sold all of the stock in the corporation that owned the inventory. That would have created a capital gain of $4,000,000, which is taxed at 15%, netting him approximately

$3,400,000. ***Improper planning cost him $1,000,000. How much do you think this program would have saved him? It's safe to say $1,000,000.***

Whenever you can sell a business, if it is incorporated longer than the minimum time needed for long term capital gains, you can sell the stock in the corporation and pay less tax.

A friend of mine owned a real estate firm. It was a DBA and he was just getting ready to turn it into a corporation. He had decided to expand the business and wanted to put $50,000 into the expansion. He asked me what would be the best way.

I explained to him that there were two common ways. One was to form the corporation and put $100,000 in as equity, and the other was to form the corporation and put the $100,000 in as a loan. The equity way would give the corporation a financial statement that the company had a net worth of $100,000. The loan did not give the corporation any net worth, however, it did allow the corporation to have the capital it needed with $100,000 of operating capital on the books.

He told me he thought the company would earn $100,000 in a year and wanted to know what would happen if he wanted to take that money out of the company. I told him, if he put it in as a loan, he could take the $100,000 back out of the company and there would only be taxes due on the interest he earned (about $1,000). Now, if he put it in as capital, and the company earned $100,000, the company would be taxed on that at the prevailing rate (about 35% or $35,000). If he wrote himself a check for the remainder, $65,000, he would be taxed on that at his personal tax rate (approximately 35% or $22,750), which would net him $32,250. He decided to put it in as a loan.

Money Invested As:	Equity	Loan	Berman Differential Added Value*
Amount Put In	$100,000	$100,000	
Amount Earned	$100,000	$100,000	
Company Tax	$35,000	0	
Personal Income Tax	$22,750	0	
Interest Paid	0	$1,000	
Money Kept	$42,250	$99,000	$57,750*

* The Berman Differential Added Value is the potential Dollar-Value-Difference of doing business one-way over another

These are just two examples of proper planning. It's best to sit down with your accountant and run all your ideas past him prior to doing large transactions so you can best structure them to your benefit.

Almost everywhere I go each day is related to business, whether it is traveling, dinner, or some other form of entertaining. When you own your own business, you get to write off a substantial portion of those expenses. This helps make up for those long hours. When I worked for a company as an employee I was never allowed to take a business deduction for going to dinner with a co-worker and our wives. When I ran a company with many employees, I took out my top management and their wives quite frequently and that was an allowable expense at the time.

International Business

Do you know the definition of a business expert? It is someone from out of town. Now, out of the country, that's an icon. Doing business out of the country is easier than you think. With global acceptance and growth of the Internet, it is happening more and more.

Recently, I had a friend ask what I would do in a certain

international business situation, which I think is a great example of the small business owner's dilemma. He had started a web-based business to sell fishing flies (yes, there is a market for fishing flies). He had found a manufacturer of flies in Thailand. The quality of the product and the cost were extremely attractive to him. Now the company in Thailand (which could be a guy with a website and dead flies) wanted payment in advance for the flies. Then he would make the flies and send them in a few weeks. The first order was to be $5,000, which was more than the entrepreneur was in a position to lose if something went wrong.

Well, he went with his gut (something I am a big fan of) and sent the $5,000 they asked for to the company in Thailand, with whom he never had done business and didn't know anyone else who had either. Well, a few weeks later he got his flies. This is the exception rather than the rule.

When I want to partner with someone in another country, I go with two options, since it's hard to sue internationally. However, before I do anything, I check their references. I ask for a list of people from the US with whom they have done business and contact them. If they have no references that I can check, this is a **red flag** for me.

Option 1. Figure out how much you can afford to lose and order that much product. Start out slow and build up as you get a level of comfort with your business contact.

Option 2. Issue them a Letter of Credit (LOC). This is where you go to your bank and put up the entire amount of the order in cash. Your bank, in turn, issues a LOC stating they have the funds and upon delivery of the product will pay for the order. These are more commonly used overseas than you think, and are an acceptable form of payment for almost anyone. This way, if you don't get your product, they don't keep your money. In the LOC you can spell out things like delivery dates, cancellation terms, product review, etc. Ask your banker about LOC verbiage. Banks like LOCs because they will charge you a fee to use your money. **It's truly a win-win situation.**

International borrowing

Just like the United States offers financing for various types of businesses, foreign governments will fund business ventures between companies in their country and U.S. companies. When I was in the wind energy business, **the Irish government lent my company approximately $10,000,000 (without any personal guarantees from me) to buy windmills that were being manufactured in Ireland and shipped to us in the US.** Now, if I would have gone to a U.S. bank for the $10,000,000, based on our business financials, we would not have qualified. The reason Ireland financed this venture was because they were subsidizing the business in Ireland, trying to encourage U.S. companies to buy their products; in essence to bring U.S. dollars to their country.

Research the country you are doing business with to see if they offer any government financing for business ventures. The best place to research is with whomever you are doing business. Go to the government's website and read it thoroughly.

Sounds short and sweet and too good to be true? I know why, because before I did it, I never knew it could be done.

Tax advantages to international business

Many countries do not have business income taxes. Also, some are known to have business and banking secrecy laws. Some of those countries are the Bahamas, Bermuda, Cayman Islands, Switzerland, and Venezuela's ABC Islands of Aruba, Bonaire, and Curacao. There are various legal ways to set up these businesses. You should talk to a lawyer and accountant in the US, as well as in the country you pick. You can also research these countries on the Internet.

- **ABC islands:** http://embajadausa.org.ve

- **Bahamas:** http://www.bahamas.com/business/index.html

- **Bermuda:** http://www.gov.bm/

- **Cayman Islands:** http://www.gov.ky

- **Swiss tax law:** http://www.taxation.ch/engl/index.html

Bearer Bond Stock

Aruba, Bonaire, and Curacao offer to set up companies in bearer bond stock, which basically means, whoever physically holds the stock in their hands, owns the company. This can be used to transfer your ownership in a company (and its bank accounts) in a matter of seconds, should that need arise. (Again, check with local and international attorneys regarding before doing business abroad.)

Public Relations (PR) and Investor Relations (IR)

Every business owner needs to know about public and investor relations. These areas are often overlooked by the naive businessperson. PR and IR can be easily established with minimal costs or expanded to meet your growing. In order to grow even the simplest of businesses or to launch a new product, business, or service, take advantage of PR. Investor Relations also need to be set up as soon as possible if you anticipate ever having an investor. Keep in mind, even if you are not looking for investor capital today, you most likely will be in the future.

Public Relations

Public relations are efforts to establish and maintain a company's image with the public by communicating the company product, event, or other pertinent information to the media and public. This is a valuable tool and if used correctly, can help build your company or launch a product cost effectively. In this section I will tell you how to garner public attention to your company with very limited cost involved.

Investor Relations

Investor Relations for a private company begins with something as simple as providing a name, e-mail address, contact page, or link on your website and a dedicated phone number for investors or potential investors to use to request information on your company. Private companies are not required to have an IR department; however, if you have investors or ever intend to have investors, you should strongly consider setting one up.

Once you become a public company, you are required to do more. The duties involved are following a policy of full and open disclosure and dissemination of a company's relevant information, favorable and unfavorable, on a consistent basis to the company's investors and the financial community. All public companies should have an IR department, either an outside IR firm hired to provide investor relations service, or they should have their own internal employees dedicated to this task.

Sometimes public relations' and investor relations' activities cross over each other and work hand-in-hand. I will try to differentiate the two.

In the chapter "Creating an Image," we explained how to create a corporate package. Now, how does that chapter's content apply to public relations and or investor relations? You need to have a corporate package to submit to the press and potential investors and other interested parties to lend your company credibility.

You can pay for ads in magazines or newspapers, or other forms of media. They can be effective, but that is not what this chapter is about. Ads are good, but when you can get stories written about you or your company, they tend to be far more effective than ads.

Public Relations Strategies

My company was advertising in a regional magazine. I noticed that each month on the cover of that magazine they featured a local business owner's picture and a few pages in a story about the company. I also noticed some of those companies had regular feature ads in the magazine. I went to my sales rep and pitched him on my company's story. I didn't say it, but I implied that for my firm to continue to advertise in his magazine, we should be featured. Nothing ventured, nothing gained. Two months later my company was featured on the cover of the magazine. We got about 25-50 times as much response from that than our paid-for ad campaign.

I had the article reprinted and added it to our company's corporate package, and it lent us additional credibility. Now this can work with local newspapers, trade publications, etc., so anywhere you advertise, pitch your story. Newspapers need a constant flow of articles to keep them going. When people ask me how that story came about, I simply tell them the magazine was looking for business stories and wrote one on us.

Another example is the time I made an agreement with a small magazine, whose reader base had strong possibilities as buyers of my company's products. Instead of advertising, I negotiated purchasing $10,000 worth of reprints of a story that they wrote about us if they put us on the cover. We sold over $1,250,000 of a high-gross margin product to that article's readers. It was a worthwhile expense. Not to mention, I still use the article in my corporate package.

Press releases are a great door opener. If you are public, you have to issue them anyway. I have seen companies attract management, secure new strategic relationships, sell their products, and gain investors as a direct result of press releases. Press releases usually cost from $75 - $1,000 however international and multi targeted releases can cost as much as $6,000 to release, based on the amount of words and the area you want covered.

If you do not know how to write a press release or even if you already know how, try this tactic: Look on the Internet for large companies in your targeted field and look at their press releases. For example, if I were planning to do an art auction on the Internet, I would look at www.ebay.com. I would pull up a year's worth of their press releases. Look for industry information and statistics that you can verify and that you can use. For people unfamiliar with press release writing, you can go to www.businesswire.com and look at other companies' releases. You may also check out releases as they are posted on Yahoo! Finance. Business Wire has a direct feed with them. Go to: http://biz.yahoo.com/bw/. Other sites where press releases are posted include: http://bigcharts.marketwatch.com/, http://cbs.marketwatch.com/, and http://finance.lycos.com/qc/. I had one client company that was once a startup in a giant industry. They had an agreement to buy a product from a large company, mark it up, and resell it. They had a good product at a good price. They wrote a press release challenging a few Fortune 500 companies to meet their product price. That press release, because it challenged the big companies, was picked up nationwide and drove thousands of people to their business, therefore becoming the springboard for what turned them into a $20 million-a-year company in a short time. The release generated so much attention that other nationally-known media picked up on it, wrote stories, and a snowball effect was created. In fact, one Fortune 500 company's vice president called the tiny startup to solicit a position with them. He became their chief operating officer for several years.

Investor Relations Strategies

Get the caller's name, rank, and serial number right from the get go. It costs a lot of money to make your phone ring with an interested party or investors. I like to calculate how much time and money I spend each quarter on marketing and public relations. Then I come up with lead costs. Let's say I spent $10,000 in a quarter and got 500 good leads. That is an average cost of $20 a lead. Now when your phone rings, consider that it cost $20 to make it ring and each call needs to be properly handled. I am not going to tell you how to train your receptionist, but I will make a few suggestions on how to handle investor relations calls.

If you set up your own internal investor relations division or department, here are a few rules. *Let's start with building your database. Every call costs money—some are worth big money. Build your database. Get the picture?*

1. **Here is how I like to answer calls: The receptionist answers the call with your pre-arranged greeting. The Investor says, "I would like to get some information about investing in your company." First, have the receptionist get his or her name and phone number (in case no one is available in that department). Once she obtains the contact information, she passes the call to the dedicated IR person.**

2. **Investor relations personnel should obtain the following information: Where did the potential investor hear about your company? Is he or she a current shareholder or a potential one? If your caller already is a shareholder, find out when the shares were bought. That way you know how much was paid a share, and if**

he or she is a satisfied customer or not, depending on the price or value of your stock the day they bought it, versus its price today.

3. Next, ask what type of information he or she seeks. You may e-mail, fax, or mail it, but before you decide how to send it, ask for your caller's physical address, then get an e-mail address. Remember, your prospect called you and want you to give away free information.

4. OK, you think you know your caller now? Think again. This person could own 100 shares bought at $3 or could own 200,000 shares. This is a delicate area, but I like to find out how big of an investor I have on my hands and delicately ask how many shares he or she owns (without sounding like I am reading a script). Most people like to brag about how much money they have, so don't be surprised if they tell you. A member of my IR teams used to say "buyers are liars," but if you don't ask, you will never know.

5. So your caller only owns 100 shares, do you look at him or her as a small fry? Not necessarily. The next question is a great one. "So, Mr. Jones you bought 100 shares of our stock back when it was $3. How much do you usually invest in companies like ours?" The answer could be that he bought 100 shares in his kid's account and has $1,000,000 to invest in companies like yours.

6. What if your prospect owns 100,000 shares? Think you have a good lead? Possibly. However, these 100,000 shares could comprise your caller's entire investment portfolio: one stock and they have no more cash. A good question to ask here is, "What percentage of your investing portfolio is that, Mr. Jones?"

7. Now you can send them the information. But what do you send? Everything that was requested, but be aware

that it costs $2-$25 for a corporate package. A good IR professional learns who he is talking to and tries to eliminate sending unnecessary expensive packages through the mail. E-mail and fax are very efficient.

You should store all information obtained from IR inquiries in a database. There are a lot of reasons for tracking your callers; one of the most important is that you now have a pre-existing relationship with each caller, so that in the future, when you go out to raise money for your company, you may be able to solicit him or her for an investment. If you have an investment banker working to raise money for you, when you tell him you have a database of people who have expressed interest in your company and have collected the above information, watch his jaw drop and tongue hit the floor!

The transition from a private company to a public company is a tremendous undertaking; however, once a company has made the decision to go public it is important to begin acting like a public company as soon as possible. Many companies invest millions of dollars each year to market their products or services to the public while only dedicating a fraction of that amount to market their company through an effective IR program. Attaining optimum market valuation of their stock and maximizing shareholder value can reinforce the value of a company's strengths and key executives through a well-conceived and well-educated IR program.

The objectives of an investor relations firm for newly public companies should focus on the very basic objectives of an Investor Relations (IR) program.

- **Define the company's corporate message and target investors;**

- **Establish a consistent and accurate communications**

> **procedure to the public and investors; and**

- **Commit, at every level of management, to the IR program's procedures and goals.**

Once a basic IR program is established, companies can continue to support investor awareness and fair market valuation of their stock by more aggressive IR campaigns.

Oh, You Got a Website. Who Cares?

The content of this chapter comes from spending almost two years working 60+ hours a week and spending millions of my own and investors' dollars as head of an Internet- based business website.

Time after time, hopeful entrepreneurs have ideas for a website and think they're in business. It's not a bad start, but you've got a long way to go (don't order that new car yet). Then there is the person who has only a Web page and thinks he is in business. *Some websites are nothing more than a brochure.* Moving the bar up a bit, you have the entrepreneur who actually builds a complex website that actually functions as a B2B (business to business) or B2C (business to consumer) website.

First, let's talk about the different kinds of websites. *The brochure style Web page can be a cost effective tool if used appropriately. These can be built for as little as $1,000 - 10,000.* Don't overpay for a website and don't build more than you need.

Printing is expensive, especially in color. If you use your website only as a brochure, a good quality brochure page can be built inexpensively and costs less than continuing to print brochures. Expenses associated with a brochure-style website are related to graphics more so than programming.

Independent website developers charge for each page or link they build. I recently paid $100 per page link. A page or link is what shows up on the screen each time someone clicks anywhere on your website. So when you plan your website, a little forethought into how much information you want to display can save you a lot of money. Call around and ask "how much do you charge per page or link?" If you already have graphics for your company you will save more.

Now here is where the money adds up. B2B and B2C websites get expensive. I built a very complex combination B2B and B2C website. The company I started paid approximately $250,000 to build it. I learned an unforgettable and expensive lesson on website development. Keep in mind that this occurred during the height of the Internet craze. Today's rates are substantially lower. Here are some tips to keep in mind when planning a website:

1. **Do not over-build or over-engineer your website.**

2. **Do not add features you don't need.**

3. **Know whether your Web firm has internal developers or if they outsource the work. Many U.S. based web firms outsource their developers from countries like India and Pakistan. When firms hire developers in other countries you will see things like even the simplest questions or change take a day (when it's only five minutes work) for an answer or repair because of the different time zones.**

4. **Pay as you go and have penalties for delays caused by the developer.**

5. **Test, test, test. Hit every button on that website yourself. Use every feature before you release it to the public. If your website malfunctions when you first launch it, you can bury your future.**

Okay, it's built, now what? Sit there and wait for people to show up? It doesn't work that way. If you have a brochure-type website you're only using for existing customers and to point people to, you may not need to market it. Or, if someone gave you millions of dollars to start print and television ads, congratulations! If you are a startup or a firm without a genie in a bottle, you will have to work at getting users to find your website.

Least expensive first, press releases. You can use a national news wire service (Business Wire www.businesswire.com) to write a press release, spend a few hundred dollars, and hope it gets picked up (see chapter on press release techniques). This is actually a very useful tool. I had a client that went from startup to over 10 million in annual sales in just over a year, gaining clients through making press releases.

Chat rooms. There are many chat rooms on the internet that chat about a plethora of topics. You can hire someone to go into these rooms and talk about your company and its products.

Banner swapping and trading. You can go to someone in a synergistic business that doesn't compete with you and make a deal to put a banner ad or link on their website to yours and you put a link on your website to the theirs.

E-mail blasts. You can really get people mad at you here if you aren't careful. Utilize an e-mail list company and rent a list that matches your criteria. Make sure the list is an opt-in list, and at the bottom of your list, have a single click to "remove me from the list" button. Opt-in means that the people receiving the e-mail have requested this type of information somewhere before.

Test Marketing

More money can be saved by test marketing. The best way to describe test marketing is when you either attempt to sell a product that you haven't finished developing, or you roll out a small marketing campaign and see your response percentage.

Let's start with a product you haven't developed yet. *My favorite way to sell something is the "takeaway." The "takeaway" is when you simply tell someone they may not qualify to buy your product, you may run out if they don't order quickly, or it's not for sale yet, etc.* I will use my latest product as an example.

You're obviously reading my book, so what I did is working. My marketing plan went as follows. Before I even finished my product, my staff began calling small business owners (which are my bread and butter) to test market using the "takeaway" system. The call went like this:

"Hello, Mr. Smith, my name is Bob Jones with **'The Berman Differential,' which is a all encompassing Business Growth and Funding System.** I am not trying to sell you anything today. Our system is not even available to business owners at this time; however, it will be available in the near future. If I could just have two minutes of your time, we both can determine if our company can help you grow, make more money, or finance your business. 'The Berman Differential' contains a database of business and legal forms, with fill-in-the-blanks, so companies can add in their own information when needed; direct links and contact information to all sorts of investment sources in every industry; business plan and presentation templates that have been proven to raise millions of dollars, and a complete book of business strategies from Bruce A. Berman, who has made millions of dollars many times over as an accomplished entrepreneur, CEO."

This test marketing activity proved the viability of our product. Not only did our grass roots marketing campaign show us this product made sense, but people were eager to offer us useful insight as to what would make it better. However, the best part of this low-cost, highly effective test was the information we attained on the customers that were interested in our product.

Because of this test we built relationships with prospective clients, accepted their input, and implemented their most common suggestions. This gave our prospects a sense of commitment to the product and a feeling of obligation to purchase it.

Not every product can be tested this simply. An effective way to determine how big your product can be is to think small. When you launch a new product advertising dollars generally equal 50-60% of a company's marketing costs. If you isolate that cost into a small area (like a city or a county), you can launch an accurate test with a significantly smaller cost. This will not only be a good indicator of your product's chance for success, it will allow the opportunity to make changes that might have been overlooked in developing your advertising materials. It also will give you invaluable, proven statistical information on the response level to your advertising campaign.

For instance, if your advertisement was launched in an area of 1,000,000 people with a per-capita income of $45,000 a year, in a magazine that reaches 100,000 people, and 2,000 people bought your product because of the ad, then you would have a 2% response from your ad. If your ad cost $20,000 and the money you received from the 2,000 orders was greater than the cost of the product plus the $20,000 ad, you made a profit. God bless you. Your idea has just proven itself. You have also learned that an area of 1,000,000 people, with a per-capital income of $45,000 a year, advertising to 100,000 people will bring an estimated 2% response. That becomes a real estimation and something on which to base future rounds of funding. ***Remember, everyone***

wants to do business with a winner and you can only become a winner once you leave the world of the thinkers and enter the world of doers. Test marketing can help you identify a winning idea at minimal cost. If 10 buyers showed up as a result of your $20,000 ad, then it's time to rethink your product or the type of marketing you're doing.

Strategic Alliances

Strategic alliances are one of the most cost-effective ways to grow your business. What is a strategic alliance? It is a business relationship between you and another business provider or consultant. Here is a simple example. While I was writing this book, I hired a company to resurface and put an epoxy coating on my garage floor. After they completed the project, the salesman for the company noticed that I did not have built-in garage cabinets, just portable plastic shelving. He told me he had a company he could refer me to that could build them for me. He also had a relationship with a company that upgraded and replaced garage doors.

These three companies are strategic partners with each other. Each of them spends marketing dollars to attract customers. Chances are that once any of them completes their project they could refer the other one. Now, this is a win-win deal. They each refer business to one another and probably for a finder's fee. What a great way to grow a business.

I have had many strategic relationships in my business career. In my business development field I come across companies that need accountants, lawyers, banks, financing sources, management personnel, graphic artists, technology development, etc. It is very common that the businesses to whom I have referred clients return the favor by doing work pro bono for me, referring me clients, and paying me finder's fees.

Strategic alliances can also be used to lend your company credibility. If you can offer your clients a broader array of services and you are a lesser-known firm, the fact that you align yourself with older, established companies gives you an air of being a more developed business. Businesses are always looking for inexpensive and effective ways to grow their companies and are more likely than you think to enter into these arrangements.

When I put a corporate identification package together for myself, I don't always list the name of my strategic partners. Sometimes I just list the services they offer. I make my determination with each business venture depending on how I get paid from my clients and the competition sensitivity. The old saying, **"it's not what you know, it's who you know,"** can be very true.

PART FOUR
{ You Can't Get the Money If You Don't Do Your Homework }

My single most important catch phrase is, "you can't get the money unless you do the homework." Over and over I have seen clients and business owners try to raise money before they did the homework. They almost always fail.

To substantially increase your chances of getting funded, read, reread, study and implement everything you have learned in this book (that's the homework). If you skipped a section go back and read it now.

This next section is about raising money and possibly going public. Remember, most investors only invest in companies that plan to go public. There are other options for investors, and I explain them in this section but they are the exception, not the rule.

The Art of Raising Money

Learning how to raise money is probably why a large percentage of you bought this book, at least that is what my business experience tells me. If you skipped ahead to this chapter and did not read all the previous chapters, I suggest, before you even think about raising money, that you go back and read this book in order from front-to-back starting at the table of contents. **"You can't get the money if you don't do your homework."** I say this to everyone who asks me about raising money. What is the homework? It is forming your company correctly, packaging your company correctly, structuring your offering in a manner that is attractive to the potential investor, preparing a proper business plan, having a management team in place, exhausting all forms of conventional financing before diluting your company, putting together strategic relationships, and putting together an investor relations and public relations plan.

Get the drift? OK, the bad news first. Those are just a few of the things you must do before you try to raise money if you want to be successful. The good news is that this book will tell you how to do those things and more. How do I know it will? Well, I have done exactly what I am explaining to you in this book time and time again successfully. I am not telling you what to do. I hate hypocrites. I am explaining exactly what I have done successfully in my own career and am passing on to you the benefit of my years of experience. To make it even easier for you, I developed a computer software program to go along with this book which can be found at my website www.BruceABerman.com.

Okay, you have done your homework. Now what?

Well, let's start at the beginning with your first offering. What you need to be careful of here is to raise the right amount of money—not too much and not too little. I like to raise money using what I call a **web of financings**. Your first offering is going to be the most expensive. It hopefully will be the lowest price per share that you will sell your shares at to raise capital. If you use your capital from the first round wisely, generally the next round of financing receives a higher valuation (price per share goes up). The reason is that if you are out to raise money, it's probably because you plan to expand your business. As your business expands, usually you get a higher valuation and, in turn, dilute your company less to raise money.

Friends and family

Your first offering is commonly known as the friends and family offering. There are three reasons:

1. One, they are great guinea pigs. If they won't invest money in your company and they know you and have followed your progress, why would a stranger invest in your company? They will be a great source of suggestions on things that need to be addressed or changed before you go out to the public. It is easier to make changes to something when you show family and friends than the public. When you go out to the public, you need to be thoroughly ready for all objections as they come at you.

2. After you get the feedback from your friends and family, you can decide to pull the offering and restructure it based on the feedback you received, without creating a bad image with the investing public or an investment firm.

3. Lastly, so your friends and family don't get mad at you. Why would they get mad at you? This is a great sales pitch if you say something to them like. **"I am offering you a chance to invest in the first round of financing in my company. If you don't want to invest, no problem, but I don't want you coming back to me mad because I didn't offer**

you this first round of financing. If my company becomes public and my stock goes up in value, you can't say I didn't offer you the first shot at my stock." I call that the "takeaway."

Imagine this scenario. Your company goes public. In your first round of financing each $1 invested is worth one share of stock and two warrants at $3 per share. Then your stock goes public at $10, which means for every $1 a friend invested he would have made $24 (I will explain how that works later). Now if you didn't offer your friends a chance to get in that first round, I guarantee they are going to be mad at you; however, they will still be your friends because you are now rich. Please be aware in most cases you are not allowed to project the future price of your stock but you can use hypothetical analogies.

What if I am not comfortable raising money from family and friends?

If you are not comfortable raising money from family and friends, don't raise any money!!! Something is wrong!!! It is that simple. The last thing you want to do is raise money for a company that you are not 125% convinced is going to be successful. If you don't believe in what you're doing, why should anybody else? Don't think you are going to be able to fake it because it will blow up on you later. If you are not 125% convinced you've got a winner, go back and rethink what you're doing. Reread this book and follow its suggestions. Put the suggestions into action. If you still don't feel 125% convinced your project is going to be successful, then it's probably going to be a loser.

How much do I raise?

That's a tough one. Not too much, not too little. With that said, here's what I recommend. *You need to raise enough*

money for your business to take a good jump forward.
This is where it gets tricky. A typical situation is that you
decide to raise $1,000,000 in your first round. You show it to
your friends and family and they all say, "I like the plan. Let
me know when you have raised about $750,000 and then I
will invest."

No one wants to be the first investor. Also, investors believe if
you have an offering to raise a fixed sum of money, and you don't
raise the whole amount called out in the offering, your business
will fail. Unfortunately this happens all the time. So what do you
do? First of all, make a list of everyone you know and what you
think they are capable and willing to invest and factor them in
your friends and family offering. If that number were $450,000,
then I would suggest rethinking your business plan and see where
$450,000 will get you. If you can move your business forward
with $450,000, then you have a reasonable plan and goal.

You may think it logical to make your friends and family offering
for $450,000. You could, however, encounter the same problem I
mentioned before, "Call me when you get to $350,000." A
possible game plan is to prepare to put out an offering for
$300,000 and in the fine print add, **"Company has the right to
oversubscribe this offering by 50%."** This disclaimer means
you can raise up to $450,000 with that document but the average
investor looks at that document as if you are trying to raise only
$300,000.

**You're not ready yet, so don't date your offering or let it
loose.** There are securities laws against "pre selling an offering,"
however, you are allowed to get "exposure" and "create interest in
your company." Go to your best possibilities and get a feel for how
much they will invest. Ask them to do you a favor and see if they
are willing to make a quick decision once they get the documents.
For example, if you have a document where you are trying to
raise $300,000, and the first week you raise $100,000, you can

create a sense of urgency (a reason to act fast) for other investors.

Once the document is printed, ***make the date on the offering the day you intend to ship out the offerings, not the date you composed the document.*** If you released the offering on May 1st and the document was dated Jan. 1, it would give the impression that you have been trying to raise money for three months and hadn't raised a penny; therefore, giving the impression that this is a bad investment.

OK, the offering is printed. Send them all out by courier so that they have to be signed for by the intended recipient or personally deliver them. This accomplishes many things; it creates a sense of importance to the document, indicates time is of the essence, and begins creating a reason for you to follow up. Wait one day and call each recipient to see if the document was received. Ask for any referrals they may have for you. ***I always ask for two-three referrals.*** This is one of the most effective and cheapest forms of marketing out there. At this point, I would call back all the people who expressed willingness to be that first investor. If you can't raise $100,000 in the first week or so, your offering may not fly. Remember a few paragraphs back? You were going to raise $1,000,000. See the importance of being prepared?

The Pitch

Before you start pitching people, you need to prepare your objection eliminating strategies. Your first step, though, is to get checks in hand. Those first few investors are critical to your success. Upon verbal interest in the offering, you are ready to go. Here is an example.

"Hi Uncle Bob, did you get my offering?" Great, well so far so good. "I received $75,000 in checks so far and have verbal commitments for about another $100,000. I am very pleased with the response I am getting." Next tell him about the company and the offering. This approach will go much better than, "Hi, Uncle Bob. Did you get my $1,000,000 offering dated three months ago? I haven't raised a penny yet. Want to send me some money?"

Uncle Bob should be impressed if you use the first tactic, rather than the latter. But if he gives you the old ***"Well, if it's going so well, you don't need my money,"*** what do you do? Give him the old "takeaway." "Uncle Bob, I don't want you to miss this opportunity and then later have you get mad at me when I can no longer sell stock at these prices. Plus, Uncle Bob, I would really like your support, and I know if you own part of the company your input could really help me."

Sex and Sizzle—Create a No-Doze Presentation

Performing a thorough and effective presentation can be the difference between a funded business and a bankruptcy filing. As stated, one of the most prevalent reasons companies fail is due to lack of capital. One of the reasons companies lack capital is because of management's inability to present a company's vision to the investment community in an attractive way.

When I give a presentation to investors, I use terms and tactics that grab and keep everyone's attention. This is done in order to gain and hold the investor's interest and keeps them from blowing up over negligible negative points, which are inevitable. Get comfortable using terms that represent sex and sizzle; point out to your investors that you're in a $200 billion industry, your company is in place to get a sizable share of that $200 billion market, there is virtually little competition, all barriers to entry have been eliminated, and companies in this industry have been receiving public valuations of 50 times projected earnings. In the Internet days, companies were unrealistically valued at 1,000 times potential earnings. This gets their juices flowing.

The Road Show

The "road show" is more of an investment banker term but investors use it too. A road show is basically where you get a group of potential investors together and put on a presentation about your company. Generally, you either rent a large presentation room at a hotel or have it at your place of business if it has capabilities to hold enough people.

Who do you get to attend the road show?

Anyone who has expressed interest in your company attends the road show. Your family and friends and all their referrals are welcome. I do not make a practice of inviting people to the road show who have already invested. Sometimes they hear something in the road show that causes them to reconsider their investment. In some cases investors attend a road show and invest more money; however, my experience is for every $1 gained by having existing investors at road shows, $2 is lost. I am a big fan of graciously leaving to the next appointment and depositing the check ASAP.

I always like to have a few people attend the road shows that are ready to invest and have already been briefed on the opportunity. No one wants to write the first check at a road show, but if you have someone who is ready, having him or her say, "I have heard enough, can I invest now?" is the best closing tool.

There are three steps to developing and executing your presentation:

1) Building the stage

This is where attention to detail counts most. You don't just put together some slides and numbers, talk for 30 minutes and then take questions. This step is much more fun. However, be careful not to fill it with too much glitz and glamour, as it can end up looking more like there are no business fundamentals other than an exciting business opportunity. To gain and keep trust and interest, you must find the delicate balance between an attractive vision and accurate, honest information when attempting to communicate your ideas in a business presentation.

Prior to having the road show, call to confirm who is attending. You want the facility where the road show is held to be a few chairs short of how many people you expect. If you expect 30 potential investors, have 20 chairs set up and another 10 chairs nearby to bring in if you need them. You want to have a bar and plenty of appetizers. You do not want your investors hungry because it tends to shorten people's attention span and contribute to a poor attitude. Plus, a few drinks never made an investor less likely to invest. Make sure the room is well air-conditioned, preferably between 68 and 70 degrees. This keeps people alert. Have you ever been to a Casino in Las Vegas that was warm and stuffy?

People need things they can feel and touch, not just see. You are going to need a slide show presentation, which will be covered a little later. First, what do you have that an investor can feel and touch during the presentation? A few things that have impressed me during presentations are recent news articles on the company or industry with supporting statistics. Printed copies of logos, owned URLs, and pictures of facilities lend credibility. Small, workable models of your vision can be useful, three-dimensional, instruments that make it easy to describe and refer to when explaining the simplicities of your Prototypes and sketches of your vision also work well.

Don't forget your attire. You don't want to look broke or that this is your first time raising money. When people put money into a company, they want to feel as if their investment is small to you or not even needed. Make sure your staff, or any consultant who is a part of the presentation, knows what to wear. Uniformity is key.

2) Slide Show 101

Creating Your Slide Show Presentation

When you have your first road show or presentation, one of the easiest and most effective tools is a Power Point presentation. There are a variety of software programs available for you to create your Power Point presentation.

Once you have selected a software program to create your presentation, you are ready for the next step. I recommend the presentation software I designed, which is available at www.BruceABerman.com. The content and delivery are the most important items in your presentation. Pictures and graphs are nice, but you must get your message across easily. I have seen hundreds of different companies' slideshow presentations and created many of my own. I believe there is an art to keeping people's attention spans during slide show presentations as well as the cohesive flow of pertinent information. For those of you who don't own my software program, "The Berman Differential," I have outlined my presentation formula for you.

Slide 1: Contains the company logo and name of founder/CEO

Slide 2: Company logo and name and title of any other officers present

Slide 3: Picture of company's main product/products

If your company were a Web-based business, you would want to display the most active page of your site. If your company sells golf clubs, display your best golf club or set of clubs, etc.

Slide 4: Company vision

In this slide you would want to describe (in 1-3 sentences) what the company is about and the image you are trying to portray.

Slide 5: The idea

In one sentence describe what inspired the company's formation, follow it with 5-7 points on the needs your company intends to fill or conveniences it will add to your prospective clients.

Slide 6: Introduction

This slide should be a brief history of the company and its current stage of development. You should have 8-10 points that would describe when the company was founded and by whom, important upcoming events, and any previous funding.

Slide 7: Management

List your top officers and their positions, plus a few sentences about their talents and duties.

Slide 8: Business overview

Using 6-10 bullet points, describe any key technologies, designs, or strategies that are the foundation of your business.

Slide 9: Affiliates

In this slide list the types and name of companies with which you are doing business. The bigger they are the better.

Example: If you were a firm that sold software to financial companies:

- **Financial Services**

    1. Bank of America

    2. Prudential

    3. Solomon Smith Barney

- **Product Development Affiliates**

  1. Microsoft

  2. Dell

  3. IBM

Slides 10 and 11: Free services and fee services

Depending on your company type, you may only provide one type of service; however, be sure to list (in bullet points) all the services available to your customers that you provide.

Slide 12: Operations

Explain how your company works. Write a few sentences describing the basic fundamentals. Start this slide with a header stating the number of parts into which the company's operations will be broken. Follow this statement with one or two sentences on each part

Slide 13: Revenues

Here you describe how your company derives its revenues. Show all your strong points. Profit margins, growth rate, etc.

Slide 14 Conclusion

Five bullet points of the most important reasons to invest in your company.

3) Walk Them Down A Road

First, look at your audience. If you are presenting a friends and family offering, depending on your friends and family, it will probably be a more comfortable setting and you might not want to overdo it. Your friends and family know you, love you, and will most likely find something wrong with everything you do (like

99% of the families out there). However, if your presentation makes sense, is workable, and well thought out, there is a good chance they will invest if they were ever serious about investing in the first place.

Now, if you are presenting to potential investors who don't know you very well, or at all, your presentation must be impeccable, because there is a very small margin of error when communicating with the investment community. One wrong guesstimate, inaccurate piece of information, or serious fumble and all could be lost. The worst thing you can do is damage your name before you even get started.

OK, here is the delicate part. Your objective should be to relay accurate information in a timely, informative, and stimulating manner.

The first thing to do is make them feel a part of the presentation. How is that done? Quickly introduce yourself and the members of your staff. When you are speaking, make eye contact with your audience, one person at a time. This gives them the feeling that you are speaking directly to them. I like to use the "SEE" rule: smile, eye contact, and enthusiasm. Remember when we talked about humans as a herd of animals? Well, so are investors. You are going to want them as calm and comfortable as they can be. If you notice someone getting bored, constantly looking at his watch or appearing uncomfortable in any way, pay special attention to that person using the "SEE" rule. You will be surprised how a calm smile, eye contact, and a little enthusiasm can bring someone's interest back. If you let one person drift too far off, the rest will soon follow. Most importantly, don't forget to breathe.

ABC—always be closing

Ask for the check. You have nothing going into the conversation and if you don't ask for the check now, you're never going to get one.

Road show tips

Here is a punch list of items to be prepared for during the road show.

1. **Your offering document. Pencil and paper for notes.**

2. **A Power Point presentation on your company (which basically just walks people and yourself through the offering). A slide show properly put together helps you in delivering your pitch.**

3. **Introduce your staff and have them available to explain specific questions. They also make good seat and room fillers until investors show up.**

4. **Facilities reserved and food and beverage confirmed.**

5. **Call all invited attendees and ask them if they are bringing anyone with them.**

6. **Answer all questions at the end of your presentation.**

Potential road show situations

1. **Hecklers.** It seems at every road show there is one person who just wants to bust your chops. He asks question after question and attempts to derail you. This person is not going to invest no matter what you say. The way to avoid this situation is to know who you invited and don't invite people you know who have that attitude. Although you asked for referrals, it's usually the referrals that are the hecklers. When I feel someone is starting to turn the room, I have only a few choices. Say to the heckler, "You have great questions but is there anyone else who has a question I can answer?" Answer those questions, and when you are done answering non-abusive questions, close the presentation and say to the heckler, "I really appreciate your questions and would like to

spend some individual time answering them. Please give me your number, and I will set up a personal appointment for you, but this is all the time I have now." Most hecklers are bullies and/or egomaniacs and they don't want to meet you one-on-one.

2. **No one asks any questions.** No matter how well a job you did, people should have questions. Hopefully there is someone in the audience asking questions to which you know the answers that are favorable to the company. Remember, this is the friends and family offering.

3. **How do I know if an investor is qualified to invest and how much I should ask him or her to invest?** First, let me tell you about what type of investors are usually the most demanding and what type of investors cause you the most problems if the company doesn't go as planned. Investor A invests $250,000 and Investor B invests $5,000. Who causes the most problems? Investor B is the biggest pain. Investor A is a big boy, and he is going to be your biggest supporter. No matter how rich an investor is, $250,000 makes them think. When someone has a large investment in a company, he tends to work with management if the company has problems. They realize the only way they have a chance of recovering their money is to work with you. Investor B shouldn't invest in the first place. Typically, investments in companies are in increments of $25,000 (to discourage the small investor). If an investor just loves your deal, but only has a fraction of the typical offering unit, turn him down. He is going to be the guy with nothing but time to make your life miserable. He will call the CEO when things are going well and call more when things aren't going as planned.

Last, but not least, don't shoot yourself in the foot by putting all your eggs in one basket. This may be a cliché but it's good advice. I usually schedule 2-3 road shows a day for two consecutive days. If I have one bad show, I have another to make up for it. If I have a good show, I talk about it in the next show and people can see my excitement. Give people a few times and options, and confirm their attendance in advance. When you confirm, you begin the process of creating "yes" answers.

Web of financings

This is where the web starts. It is not unusual for a company to have 1-5 different money raisings prior to its IPO. They usually start out with the first financing being the most dilutive but there is one other possibility of a round that can be very costly to the business owner.

1. **Research and Development Stage—Company's First Round of Financing**

In this stage a company brings in no revenue and has yet to develop a product. For example, if a company believes it can invent a drug that would cure a specific disease, but is far away from creating the actual drug itself or getting FDA approval, they are in the research and development stage. They might have a detailed plan on how to create the drug, medical documentation proving its viability, and chemical tests that show the drug will work, but until they have the actual drug ready for use, and it passes through all governmental regulatory checks, they are in the research and development stage.

The research and development stage is one of the most dilutive rounds of financing. At this juncture you do not have a tangible product to demonstrate, which increases the risk to the investor.

Another example of first-round financing

You have an idea for a product and need money to build a prototype. This is one of the earliest stages of investment and a viable use of capital. Here you would raise enough money to complete the task at hand and the initial operating cash only. This will be a highly dilutive financing. At this stage of the business, investors prefer that the management of the company is not now taking or accruing a salary. Do not take more money than you need at this price. ***R&D first round offerings typically are from $250,000 to $1,000,000.***

2. Pre-Production Stage—Second Round of Financing

The pre-production stage is when a company has a fully developed product that has not yet been distributed to its consumers. Take the drug from the previous example. Say it has been created, passed through government regulations, and is ready to be consumed by the public that needs it, but has yet to reach the hand of its consumers. However, companies in this stage can begin to pre-sell the product to jump start the revenue-generating process.

You have a product and potential orders, and now you want to raise money for product inventory, launching the product on the market, and opening a new facility.

At this stage, the more you can document, the higher your stock will be priced. Having orders in hand shows a lot more credibility than, "We believe our product is so great they will be knocking our doors down." If you can't document your orders, the investment banker's attitude is that the orders don't exist. Being able to show how you are going to produce, distribute, and package your products is paramount. ***These financings usually are in the $1,000,000 - $3,000,000 range.***

3. Post-Revenue Stage—Third Phase of Funding

Post revenue is when you are up-and-running. Congratulations. You developed a product, people have ordered your product, and they are paying for the product. At this stage of financing, the company has eliminated much of the risk. We know the product works, consumers want it, and it can be produced at a gross profit. **These offerings are usually between $1,000,000 and $3,000,000 range.**

4. Oh no, we messed up—Fourth Stage of Funding

This truly can be your most expensive financing. Here you have raised a few million dollars and spent it. You are behind in your business plan, production costs were more than you anticipated, the product could not be sold at your target price, and the cost of distribution was more than projected. Do you still have a valid business? Yes, you do; however, you have lost major credibility with the investment community. Now, what you have going for you is the simplest rule in investing. Since he has probably provided the first two or three rounds of financing, the investment banker is in so deep he needs to keep you afloat to protect his clients' investments.

"The Investment Banker is in deep and he needs to save his investment." There is a known philosophy that once an investment banker has his investors' money in a company, he is stuck feeding that company more capital until the company makes it or dies. It really has more to do with your investment banker, how his other investments are doing, and how the market conditions are at the time, rather than your business itself, if he is going to feed you more money.

If all his other deals are soaring he may be more likely to say, "One bad deal out of four is a great return" and simply cut his losses and hope you survive without him. After all, you still have your life in this business. This is where you need to do research on your investment banker to know how bad of a position you are in. I didn't say "good" for a reason, because no matter how much you have the investment banker in a bind, the fact is, you blew it. You over-projected and under-estimated costs and you are way out of favor with the investment community. Better find a sacrificial lamb in your management team to slaughter and blame for the screw up or the investment banker will want to replace you. **These financings typically are $250,000 - $2,000,000.**

5. Pre IPO stage

If you have gotten this far, my job is almost done. *I said almost.* It's not all about going public and raising money. Don't make the mistake that once you are public everything is wonderful. When it comes to making money and wealth, the basic rule is, *"It's not what you make, it's what you keep."*

This is the stage where an investment banker becomes a company valuation expert. Investment bankers and groups of investment banking firms, called the Syndicate, do IPOs. What I can help you with is advising you on what to expect from investment bankers and how to best deal with them.

First rule

Investment bankers will call you their client. You're not. You are just a one-time customer, aka the enemy. You don't believe me? Ask anyone that has gone public a few years ago. The investment banker's main client is their investor, who invests in the company. They hope to have their investors continue to reinvest over and over in new deals as the investment baker continues to rack up fees. Their next loyalty goes to the other investment bankers in the syndicate, because they hope to do deals together for years.

From an investor's viewpoint, why are you there? It's because the investment banker has a base of investors willing to put money into companies. *You are one deal to them and then they are off to the next company.*

Second rule

Investment bankers are a necessary evil. However, armed with some of the facts in this book, you should be able to negotiate from a more informed position. Don't let them know you are on to them. They have a reputation of being egotistical—it goes with the territory. Think about their job; it mainly consists of telling high net worth individuals how to invest their money. "Go with me on this Bob, it's going to be a big winner. Didn't I make you $50,000 on my last recommendation?" That is a typical pitch an investment banker uses.

What to look for when working with investment bankers

The investment banker is going to try to convince you that your company is worth less than it is, and should be priced lower per share. Think about it. If your company is worth $15 per share and they do your IPO at $12 per share, the investors upside is only $3 per share. Oh, boy what a gain. Now if they convince you that your stock is only worth $7 per share and do your IPO at $7 and the stock goes up to $15 a share, their investors make $8 per share. Thus, over 100% gain. They are heroes to their investors, and they will try and confuse you and usually look at you and say, "Don't worry about the 2,000,000 shares you sold at $7. Think about all the shares you have left that are worth $15."

This is their MO: Make the investors happy, and get the investors as much money as they can through the sale of your stock. Oh, I almost forgot that the investment banker collects a lot of fees and stock warrants. Oh, their stock warrants are usually set around the price at which they sell your stock to the investors. So, if they sell your company's stock to their investors at $12 a share instead of $7 a share, the investment banker pays $5 per share more as well. Now do you really think he wants your valuation to be more or less?

Standard IPO fees

If you're doing an IPO with a well-known investment-banking firm, their past deals tell you a lot. First, remember all the information you want to find out is public, because being public mandates full disclosure. Look at all the companies the investment banker took public in the last year. See where the original IPOs were priced and compare it to today's stock prices. If the majority of the company's prices are up, they have happy investors, then they are in a prime position to be successful on your IPO. If their last IPOs are in the toilet, they are what we call, "blown up," and the odds aren't good of them raising money. When you're looking at the price of their offerings, check to see if I wasn't right in the last paragraph.

Now, there is more information you can get by checking their past IPOs. You can find out what they charge their client companies. Right there on page 1 it will say what they received. Typically, investment bankers charge 8-10% commission, a 1%-3% non-accountable expense, (I love that name), a syndication fee of 1%-2%, and there could be a host of other actual costs. Investment bankers also want equity. They usually require warrants to buy your stock at 10% over the price the investor paid for his stock, and the amount they request tends to be one warrant for every 10 shares of stock the company sells in the IPO. (They call them warrants at 110% for 10% of the stock sold in the offering). So, that reiterates my valuation claims. Investment bankers' fees tend to stay consistent in good markets as well as bad. Your best source is looking at their recent IPOs.

Raising money tips

Are you ready to raise money? Do you have everything in place you need? Here is a punch list.

1. **Completed business plan or offering document**

2. **Slide show presentation**

3. **Management team in place**

4. **List of potential investors**

5. **Corporate identity package**

6. **Product to demonstrate**

7. **Support documentation or facts to back up your statements**

8. **Practice the presentation on your toughest friends**

9. **Be ready to ask for the check**

10. **Be ready to ask for referrals of potential investors**

Management team

Many business owners make the fatal mistake of believing they are qualified to be the head of the management team of their company; after all, they built the company from scratch. The first thing investment bankers look for is management. Most companies are projecting to go from startup to $50,000,000 - $100,000,000 in sales within five years. Investment bankers look to see who on the company's management team has actually run a $100,000,000 company. Didn't think of that, did you? Don't feel bad, most people don't.

If you haven't run a $100,000,000 company, you need to hire someone who has been a senior level officer of one to be part of your management team. It's hard to explain, but until you have had the experience running a company that large, you just won't know how to handle certain situations. You need to put your pride and ego aside here, because if you don't, you may never get funded.

If you are planning to raise money, investors like to see a strong chief financial officer (CFO) in place. After all, this is who will be handling the money. If you are planning to be public, someone in senior management has to have experience as a senior level officer at a public company. Once again, until you have been involved in upper level management of a public company, you won't know what to expect.

I am not telling you to do anything I haven't done or am not willing to do. It's just a fact that you need to address. I have been the CEO at all my companies except for my two securities firms. I do not hold the licenses necessary to be the CEO of a securities firm, so I hired qualified personnel to hold those positions.

When I take investor money into one of my businesses, I hire a CFO who has public company experience and holds a CPA license. I am qualified to run many businesses as CEO, but by bringing in a CFO/CPA with public company experience, I put my investors at ease, as well as myself, knowing I have a competent staff. Since I have no formal education, I build my management team with as many college-educated vice presidents as I can tolerate.

The investment banking industry is a good old boys club

I don't agree with this practice; however, here are the cold-hard facts. These are not my rules but they are my observations of being involved in years of investor financings. In fact, this practice is against the law and hopefully will change one day. However, I am here to help you get funded, so I am sharing my observations.

If you're looking to raise money from investment bankers and you have females in senior level management, your job may be much harder than if you didn't. If women are listed as major stockholders in your offering document your money raise has increased from difficult to almost impossible.

I have asked different investment bankers, over the years, why it is women have such a hard time getting funded, and their responses are usually on the same lines. What I have been told is that investment bankers have a fear that if times get tough in business, women tend to have the option, more than men, of being able to rely on their spouses for financial support and are more willing to walk from a company when it is having problems. Maternity leave and the fact that new businesses fail at a very high rate compound their concerns.

Martha Stewart did it why can't I?

Martha Stewart is a prime example of the exception rather than the rule. Now for the exception rather than the rule test, can you name five other women owned and operated business that were as successful as Martha Stewart? I don't think so. But, just drive down the street, turn on your computer or television and you will see numerous successful businesses started and run by men. Based on the way Martha Stewart's company's value dropped when she was involved in a scandal, and now that she has actually been convicted of a felony, expect the road to get even tougher for women. Out of the 500 fortune 500 companies only six are led by female CEOs. Yes, there are exceptions to every rule, however, I like the path of removing any and all objections to invest and gain the highest possible odds of having a successful money raise.

What do you do if you're a woman business owner?

There is an option for women business owners and start up companies that have women holding senior level management positions. So here is what I would tell my sister to do if she were looking to raise money for a new business. I believe in taking full advantage of every aspect of a business. Businesswomen have the added advantage of applying for various minority grants and small business loans funded by the government exclusively for women entrepreneurs. I suggest thoroughly researching all of these options. Secondly, consider appointing several men to your board of directors. Even if your business sells products only used by women, if your board of directors is largely comprised of industry- experienced men, you may remove some investors' concerns.

There should be a section in all offerings that talks about stock owned by management and lists the major stockholders. I would consider placing the majority of women's stock in a family trust. Of course you must disclose the beneficial ownership of that trust but the psychological emphasis is being taken off the fact that a woman owns the majority of the company's stock.

This is where you have to make up your mind as to why you are in business. If it is to prove something to the world that women can be as successful as men—good luck raising money. If it's about raising money and building a company, then carefully consider what has been said in this section.

The Exit

Investors are always looking for their exit. An exit is when and how the investors are going to get their money back. When you raise money, it is important to evaluate which exit you plan on taking and make sure your company is properly formed (see chapter on Forming the Company) so that when you raise money, you can properly disclose to the investors what, where, how, and when their exit will happen.

Different type of offerings

If I don't want to go public, what can I offer my investors?

In most money raising the ultimate goal for the investors and the company is for the company to go public. In those cases, the most common thing to offer an investor is the opportunity to invest in its stock. There are other ways to attract investors, especially if the stock market is in an unfavorable condition.

Equity

If you are going to give equity in the company when you don't believe the company is viable to go public, then the only reason an investor would want equity is if he believes the company is going to eventually be sold or merged with a larger company. There is a common thought in the investment community that if you own 49% or 1% of a private company (unless there are side agreements), you have no control whatsoever in what the company does and the equity has little to no value to you until the company is either sold, merged, or brought public.

Profit sharing

If you have established a business as a form of a partnership or even on an equity basis, one way to entice investors is with a pre-determined profit sharing plan. For example, you can offer your investors 25% of the company profits for life if, let's say, they invest $1,000,000 in your company. Keep in mind; if you decide to go this way, you are almost certainly closing the door to ever going public. ***Going public is all about earnings per share, not who owns the stock.***

One of the pitfalls of this type of investor compensation is that it is like paying alimony for life. The investors have the right to look over your shoulder at every turn and complain about how much you spend, pay your employees, every business decision you make, etc.

Royalties

I see this in a lot of companies developing a single product. For example, someone develops a golf driver and needs $2,000,000 to launch an infomercial, so he offers $15 for every driver sold to an investor for the money. This is a good way to attract capital for a particular project.

The trickiness comes if the driver takes off and you decide to add a collection of assorted woods, irons, and other golf accessories. Your future may become limited because you are not a likely public candidate, plus how do you raise additional money now to sell your other products without co-mingling the first investors?

Loan with a royalty agreement

This can solve the above problem for you. Let's say that same golf company structured the $2,000,000 as a loan with a royalty. The investor gets the loan paid back at the rate of $15 a club, but there is a cap once the investor gets paid back his initial $2,000,000 plus an agreed-upon interest amount. The investor continues to get a royalty of $15 a club until 400,000 clubs are sold ($6,000,000), which is a three-to-one return.

The lesson here is?

Structure and pre-plan your destiny. Most entrepreneurs have great visions of building a huge business. I don't think I have met an entrepreneur with an idea that he hopes will only make $100,000; it's always millions, or some think billions. The most important thing here is to plan for the beginning to be successful and don't limit your future with improper structuring.

There is a way to un-ring the bell of improper structuring, but it is expensive, time consuming, and you can't always be sure it will get done. You can go back to your investors, if they are getting a royalty, and renegotiate with them to get equity. It usually goes something like this:

Dear Investor

Thank you for investing in our company. We appreciate your loyalty and hope you are happy with your investment. Initially, when you invested in our company, we had hoped to sell 400,000 golf clubs, which would earn you three times your original investment.

We have sold 100,000 golf clubs to date and you

have received 100% of your original investment back. We now have developed new products; a complete set of woods, including 3, 5, 7, and 9 woods, as well as an exciting set of irons and assorted golf accessories.

In order to further expand our business, we have sought the help of an investment-banking firm, which is hoping to raise $5,000,000 and take us public. Our original agreement with you for a royalty, however, precludes us from going public. It seems investment-banking firms want the earnings of their clients (us) to be as high as possible, because companies are valued on a multiple-times-earnings basis.

I believe we have good news for you and a viable alternative for all of us to prosper far greater than we originally thought. We have an offer for your consideration to convert your royalty of $15 a driver to 800,000 shares of stock in our company. Enclosed is our business plan, which projects our company post funding to be worth an estimated $10 - $15 per share. This would equate to over twice what you were expecting to receive in royalty payments in half the time.

Please consider the enclosed information. We will be holding an investor meeting on this subject in the next month, where we can get your input and answer any questions you might have.

Sincerely,

John Smith, CEO

In Conclusion

Why so much talk about going public? Because that is usually the way investors make the highest possible returns. The stock market might be flat today, but people invest for the long term. Investing, when the market is flat, can be the best time because companies are not getting outrageous valuations and by the time the company executes its business plan, the market may be soaring again.

Mechanics of Going Public

This is the event for which your investors have been waiting, and, hopefully, you too. Most investors only want to invest in companies that go public. Why, you ask? When a company goes public, the hope is that the stock the investor owns has gone up substantially in value. By being public, the opportunity is created for the investor to cash out if and when he chooses.

Benefits of being a public company

Here are some of the more common reasons companies desire to go public.

1. **Creating a priced valued currency:** Your stock will now have a more verifiable dollar value.

2. **Shareholder liquidity:** Gives the shareholders an opportunity to turn their investment in the company into cash if and when they desire.

3. **Increased valuation:** Publicly traded companies usually obtain substantially higher valuations than private companies. Valuations for public companies tend to be much higher than a similar private company.

4. **Acquisitions:** Making acquisitions with public stock are easier and generally require less cash, if any.

5. **Management recruiting:** Having a fixed value currency (stock) helps to attract top management with favorable stock options.

6. **Capital formation:** Raising capital is usually easier because of the added liquidity for the investors, and the added security investors gain from the mandatory disclosure requirements of a public company.

7. **Financial planning:** Public company stock is often easier to use in estate planning for the principals. Public stock can provide an exit strategy for the founders

If all of the above is not a priority for you, you should probably rethink your decision to go public.

Duties of being a public company

The duties of publicly traded companies are far greater in disclosing information than private companies. Some of the public company regulations mandate requirements through written documents on the company's financial position and the formation of directors and board members.

The distribution of Annual and Interim Reports

Annual Reports are audited documents required by the SEC and sent to a public company's shareholders at the end of each fiscal year, reporting the financial results for the year (including the balance sheet, income statement, cash flow statement, and description of company operations), and commenting on the outlook for the future. The term sometimes refers to the Form 10-K, which is sent along with the report and contains more detailed financial information.

Interim Reports or Form 10Q are unaudited documents required by the SEC for all U.S. public companies, reporting the financial results for the quarter, and noting any significant changes or events in the quarter. Quarterly reports contain financial statements, a discussion from the management, and a list of "material events" that have occurred with the company.

The formation of audit committees

A committee is designed to examine and verify a company's financial and accounting records and supporting documents by a professional, such as a CPA.

The formation of Independent Directors

These are individuals elected by a company's shareholders to establish company policies, including selection of operating officers and payment of dividends.

Shareholder meetings

The company must host meetings held for those who own stock in the company. For public companies, along with the ownership is a right to declared dividends and the right to vote on certain company matters, including the board of directors.

Potential drawbacks of being public

Just as being public has a benefit for companies, there are also some potential drawbacks to being public. Mainly, the drawbacks have to do with disclosure and some increased costs inherent with being public.

Disclosure

When you are a public company, you are required to report all material events in a timely manner. If your company has executed a contract with a Fortune 500 company, and the order is going to have a substantial impact on your company's financial outlook, you would most likely have to report it publicly. Now, a potential drawback is that you end up telling your competitors what you are doing, giving them a chance to try to gain an edge on you or target your order. If one of your key employees is involved in a public scandal, it can seriously impact your stock's value. Recently, a public company's stock lost billions of dollars of value because its founder was involved in a business scandal. You must report all litigation in which the company is involved. Doing so gives the people you are in litigation with a potential edge.

Costs

Almost everything costs more when you are public. Private companies have the option of not having their financial statements audited. Public companies must have audited financials. Public companies must also file quarterly and annual statements on a timely basis. Any material event must be disclosed on the appropriate reporting form. Events that require shareholder approval take more time and are a costly process. The requirement of having outside directors and setting up audit committees adds extra financial costs. Communicating with shareholders and public and investor relations must be maintained.

Greater management liability

Management is under greater scrutiny and liability when operating a public company. Your business decisions must be in the best interests of your shareholders, even if they are to your personal financial detriment. You can be held both civilly liable and criminally liable for actions taken by you or your employees.

Going public

Isn't an IPO (initial public offering) the only way to go public? No, it's not the only way. If you are at the point where you have an investment banker ready to do an IPO for you, great, but if not, look closely at these other options. Here are three other commonly used ways to become a public company; merger/acquisition, reverse merger, and the filing of a 15c211.

1. Merger/Acquisition

OK, let's say your company is private, and a public company wants to merge or acquire you. Here is an example. The already public company XYZ Corp. is trading at $5 per share and they have 20,000,000 shares issued. That would mean that they had a market value of $100,000,000. You are willing to sell/merge your company, ABC Corp., for $10,000,000. XYZ Corp. would issue you 2,000,000 of their shares (remember they are public at $5 per share) for 100% of the shares of your company. Now, effectively, you and the other owners of ABC Corp. now own 2,000,000 shares of publicly traded XYZ Corp. and the stock of ABC Corp. is retired. Obviously you have lost total control of your company, and the board of directors of XYZ Corp. is now your boss.

2. Reverse Merger/Public shell BBX

This type of merger is similar to the merger/acquisition; however, the shareholders and board of directors of your company usually remain in control. These companies are more commonly known as public shells; they are publicly traded companies looking to merge with a private company. The term "public shell" is more of an industry term than a legal definition. Companies become public shells in a variety of ways. The term "fully reporting" is an important term to look at when you consider a shell as a means to go public. If a shell is not fully reporting it is not capable of trading at the current time and may have difficulty ever becoming a reporting company or a trading company.

Merge with a company that had previously done an IPO and their business failed.

Let's say a company that did an IPO raised $10,000,000 to develop an AIDS vaccine. After spending almost the entire $10,000,000, the vaccine was turned down by the FDA; it doesn't work and has no chance of ever working. Subsequently, most of the employees quit and the original business plan of the company was aborted. Now, if the company keeps up with (having fully reported) its entire SEC mandated filings, financial reporting, and still meets the guidelines to be listed with a stock exchange, it is, in essence, a public shell.

The drawback with this kind of shell is that you have $10,000,000 worth of investors who are not happy. They invested in an AIDS vaccine and now you're merging your company, which makes spark plugs in their place. Besides inheriting a bunch of unhappy shareholders (who are anxious to sell their devalued stock as soon as you do something good), you assume any potential legal liabilities they may have. I merged one of my companies with a shell similar to this example and when I did my due diligence, saw the company I was merging with had a suit against its former president for a modest amount. I knew I would have to disclose it, but my opinion was that I would drop the suit and have a clean company with no litigation disclosures, which was the only potential liability. I dropped the suit and the former defendant cross-complained against the new entity, which was my company. So now, what I thought I had avoided, blew up in my face. These are one of my least-favorite shells.

Blind Pool shells

Parties with the sole purpose of finding a company to merge with have formed blind pool shells. Public companies, if originally formed as a blind pool (if now trading), have distinct advantages as a shell. Usually they have not conducted any business and have very few liabilities. Recently government regulators have clamped down on this practice, and new companies, trying to become public through this process, are having trouble becoming approved for trading.

Business Plan Shells

Business plan shells are publicly traded companies that became a public company by raising a little capital (usually between $25,000 and $250,000) and submitting their business plan and all the requisite forms to the SEC. Typically these types of shells, after they are approved for trading and given a symbol, discontinue their business plan and look for merger candidates. This is my favorite type of shell to go into if you want to become public quickly. They usually haven't conducted any business yet and the potential for unknown or foreseeable liabilities is less likely to exist.

Bankruptcy Shells

Bankruptcy shells are usually companies that went public, via an IPO, and later went bankrupt and have kept their trading status by staying current on their filings. Once a judge has entered a court order, these shells, effectively, may not have any liabilities. It should all be spelled out in the bankruptcy plan. The one potential drawback is that in all your future filings you will have to make a note that says ABC Corp. (now merged company name/your name) was formerly known as (DEF Corp.) and in 2003, DEF Corp. filed Chapter 11 Bankruptcy. Now the knowledgeable person will understand that you just merged with a bankrupt shell, but the unknowledgeable person will think something may be wrong. The problem is, that there are a lot of unknowledgeable investors out there.

General public shell information

Most shells are traded on the Over The Counter (OTC) Bulletin Board. The main reason is they were probably formed with insufficient capital or have lost their capital and don't meet NASDAQ's minimum listing requirements. There are NASDAQ shells; however, they are very rare. Typically, they are companies whose business plan failed; albeit, they still have sufficient capital and meet all the NASDAQ requirements to maintain their listing.

What do shells cost?

A lot. So you better be sure you want to go public. Typically, today a bulletin board shell costs between $150,000 and $400,000, and they will require, upon merger, that the old owners of the shell retain one to ten percent of the new entity.

Whose stock is tradable after a merger?

Typically the only stock freely tradable after a reverse merger is that of the shell owners. Their stock is tradable and all other stock is usually restricted. Other stock can be freed up by filing a registration statement with the SEC, or once it is one year old, by filing what is known as 144 paperwork. Any stock brokerage firm will have 144 paperwork.

3. Filling a 15c211

Filling a 15c211 is a process that is commonly done when you have an existing company currently in business with an established shareholder base from prior private money raise. If you are not in a hurry, this process can be done (if done right) in about six months. I prefer this method, if I am not in a hurry, because everyone who owns stock in this venture bought it because they wanted to invest in a company that is actually public. The process to go public this way is listed below.

In order to do a 15c211 filing, I recommend hiring a company that specializes in these filings. They usually charge around $15,000 and a few percent of the equity in the company. Here is what they will normally do for the company:

- **Conduct background checks on officers, directors, and majority shareholders.**

- **Try to identify potential red flags with the NASD.**

- **Carry out record checks, utilizing private investigators and attorneys.**

- **Perform detailed checks including information gathered from the FBI, Department of Justice (DOJ), and the SEC.**

- **Furthermore, check on civil/criminal filings, tax liens, and judgments.**

- **Locate a broker dealer to sponsor the filing.**

After they complete a thorough research on your company and the people involved, these types of firms will check every document related to the filing, page-by-page for completeness and accuracy. This is done in order to greatly reduce the amount of questions sent back by the NASD and to expedite your filing. If certain red flags are not cleared prior to the submission of your company's filing, these issues will be exposed to NASD scrutiny and put on a permanent record. In some situations, a company's filing may become permanently dead and will never clear. Even if you later decide to resubmit, you're filing through a different market maker or under a new name.

The Broker-dealers' due diligence is shared with you (the issuer) and your securities attorney. Broker-dealers typically fill out the Form 211, add their cover letter for submission, and send your filing to the NASD, most of the time with a small amount of review. They operate on the belief that everything you give them is in perfect order.

Once the NASD member firm submits the filing to the OTC Compliance Unit, the examiners are required to respond within 10 business days.

The firm would then review all NASD letters, formulate responses, and send the correspondences back to the filing broker/dealer. The broker/dealer then reviews the answer and sends the response on to the OTC Compliance Unit. The correspondence process could take as long as 2-12 months.

Comparing Three Ways to Go Public

Traditional Underwriting IPO (Initial Public Offering)

Time: 6 to 12 months

Cost: $175,000 to $500,000. The company will be out of pocket at least 50% of this amount prior to completion.

Capital: Typically raises more capital than other types of transactions.

Problems: Underwriting may be delayed or canceled. Market conditions or underwriter may change issue price.

Reverse Merger or Buy an Existing "Public Shell"

Time: 2 weeks to 120 days

Cost: $150,000 to $400,000

Capital: Does not raise money but stock is now valued and tradable.

Problems: Potential "skeletons" in acquired shell. Control shareholders of operating company may receive restricted shares.

Advantages: Typically Reverse Merger or Public Shell Merger is the quickest way to get public. Non-control investors may receive registered or trading shares.

Filling a 15c211

Time: 2 to 12 months

Cost: $15,000 to $100,000

Capital: Does not raise money.

Problems: None

Advantages: Company does not inherit another company's potential problems. Shareholder base is mostly people who are familiar with and have invested in the actual public company.

How does a Reverse Merger with a Public Shell work?

A reverse merger is a transaction whereby the private company shareholders may gain control of a public company by merging it in with their private company. The private company shareholders receive a substantial majority of the shares of the public company (normally 85% to 90% or more) and control of the board of directors. The transaction can be accomplished in as little as two weeks, resulting in the private company becoming a public company. The transaction does not have to go through a review process with state and federal regulators because the public company has already completed the process. The transaction involves the private and shell company exchanging information on each other, negotiating the merger terms, and signing a share exchange agreement. At the closing, the public shell company issues a substantial majority of its shares and the board control to the shareholders of the private company. The private company shareholders pay for the shell and contribute their private company shares to the shell company and the private company is now public.

Upon completion of the reverse merger, the name of the shell company is usually changed to the name of the private company. If the shell company has a trading symbol, it is changed to reflect the name change. An information statement, called an 8-K, must be filed within 15 days of the closing. The 8-K describes the newly combined company, stock issued, information of new officers and directors, and financial information. The financial statements must be audited to U.S. GAAP standards, and the SEC allows a maximum of 75 days to amend the 8-K with audited financials if necessary.

If the shell company is listed on the bulletin board, the registered or "free trade" shares can continue to trade. The company can do a private placement immediately. To trade new shares offered by the public, the newly combined public company must first register the shares with the SEC. This process takes two to six months and normally requires filing a registration statement with the SEC under Reg. SB-2 or SB-1.

If the shell company does not have a symbol, an application for a symbol is usually made to the NASDAQ Bulletin Board. The application for a symbol requires filing a form 15c211 by a market maker that is a member of the NASD. The Bulletin Board has no financial requirements. A listing will be granted if the affairs of the company are in order and the company answers the questions posed by NASDAQ.

Advantages of Going Public Through a Reverse Merger or a Public Shell Purchase

Less costly: The costs are significantly lower than the required costs for an IPO.

Quicker: The timeframe to do a reverse merger is much faster than any other means of going public.

Requires little track record: While an IPO requires a relatively long and stable earnings history, the lack of an earnings history does not normally keep a privately held company from completing a reverse merger.

Removes Risk: You will become public. This is unlike a scheduled IPO, which may be withdrawn due to an unstable market condition, even after most of the upfront costs have been expended. There is little doubt that you will be public when you merge with a public company.

Less Management Time: Traditional IPOs generally require greater attention from senior management.

No Underwriter Requirements: No underwriter is needed. This can be a factor to consider given the difficulty companies face in attracting an investment banking firm to commit to an IPO.

Preparation for a Reverse Merger or Public Shell Merger

Locate a Public Shell: Public shells can often be found by consulting with securities law firms or CPA audit firms that deal with public companies and the internet.

Do your Due Diligence: Due diligence on public shells cannot be over emphasized. Advice from your securities counsel, auditors, and a financial consultant should be utilized.

Finish your Business Plan: Potential investors, public shareholders, auditors, securities counsel, brokers, and market makers will want to see a well-documented business plan. Public companies need the ability to show good sales and earning growth.

Have Management Team in Place: Public investors demand strong management teams.

Financial Audits: SEC qualified audited financial statements for your last two fiscal years are mandatory.

Experienced Securities Counsel: Your attorney must be qualified to deal with regulatory compliance and the ongoing reporting requirements of all public companies. Many law firms either specialize or have partners that specialize in securities.

Public Company Experience: Your company should have at least one person in senior management who has significant public company experience. Financing consultants can often assist management in the complex issues of being a public company and maintaining a good relationship with the financial community.

Devise your financing strategy: A reverse merger does not necessarily mean you get capital. You must develop a plan for raising capital. Management must first consider how additional capital will be raised after the deal is done.

Requirements Necessary to Close a Reverse Merger or Public Shell Merger

Business plan of the company you are merging with: You will need sufficient information to complete and file the required 8-K with the SEC.

Management list: You will need all pertinent information on all the officers and directors, including completion of the "Officer and Director Questionnaire" for all officers and directors to remain once the company merger is completed.

Agreement on structure and terms of merger: A letter of intent is a good place to start.

Audited Financial Statements: For two years you must have your financial statements audited, conforming to Generally Accepted Accounting Principles (GAAP). The audit statements of the private company will have to be consolidated with the public company's financial statements.

Shareholder consent for the merger: Preferably 100% of existing shareholders of the private company are needed to merge or exchange their shares for shares of the public company.

Agreement with the officers and directors of the public shell: They are going to be replaced with the officers and directors designated by the private company merger partner. They need to agree in advance in writing to resign.

Shareholder Lists: List of all shareholders in the private company that will make the share exchange.

Share ownership: Number of shares to be outstanding "post merger," and a complete breakdown of share ownership post merger. It is often necessary for the public shell to do a reverse split and/or cancel shares owned by the affiliates of the public share prior to completing the merger.

Legal Documentation: A prepared share exchange agreement, stock purchase agreement, definitive merger agreement, and all other documents necessary to complete the merger.

SEC Documentation: Final preparation of the 8K that is required to be filed with the SEC within 15 days of closing the merger. As stated earlier, this is required to contain consolidated audited financial statements, but the SEC will allow an additional 75 days to file an amended 8K with the audited statements.

What are the different stock exchanges?

There our four basic stock exchanges. The New York Stock Exchange (NYSE), the American Stock Exchange (AMEX), the NASDAQ which has two listings, the National Marketing Systems and the Small Cap (NASDAQ:NMS and NASDAQ:SC) and the Over the Counter Bulletin Board (OTC:BB). Each exchange has its own standards, requirements, and fee structure to become initially listed on them as well as maintain your listing. For a comprehensive and updated list on all the requirements necessary to list a company, maintain a company listing, and any of the exchanges fees and rules go to our website at www.BruceABerman.com.

AMEX

The American Stock Exchange (AMEX) is the second-largest stock exchange in the U.S., after the New York Stock Exchange (NYSE). In general, the listing rules are less stringent than those of the NYSE, and thus the AMEX has a larger representation of smaller companies than the NYSE. In 1998 the parent company of the NASDAQ purchased the AMEX and combined their markets, although the two continue to operate separately.

Equity Requirements

Most of the AMEX filing requisites require shareholder equity of $4,000,000 for companies wishing to be listed. There is a variance for that if a company has either $75,000,000 in assets or a $75,000,000 market cap and can meet other criteria that a company with a net worth less than $4,000,000 can be listed. However, they are the exception not the rule. I will bet before you read this you had no idea that a company with a net worth as little as $4,000,000 could be listed on the AMEX.

Other Requirements

Depending on which of the above scenarios you meet, you will need between 400 and 800 shareholders and 500,000 and 1,000,000 shares in the public float. There is also a requirement in some cases that you must have earned $750,000 in the last two fiscal years.

NYSE

The New York Stock Exchange is the oldest and largest stock

exchange in the U.S. The NYSE, which is known as the Big Board, has the most stringent requirements for companies to be listed. Unlike some of the newer exchanges, the NYSE still uses a large trading floor in order to conduct its transactions. In order to facilitate the exchange of stocks, the NYSE employs individuals called specialists, who are assigned to manage the buying and selling of specific stocks.

Financial Requirements

Unlike the AMEX that requires only a minimum of 400 to 800 shareholders, the NYSE requires a minimum of 2,000. A public company's market cap must be $100,000,000 on the NYSE.

You need either pre-tax earnings of $6,500,000 over the last three years or $4,500,000 in the most recent year. Should you not meet those earnings requirements, if you have cash flow of $25,000,000 for the last three years, or $100,000,000 in revenues in the most recent year, you may qualify for an exemption.

NASDAQ

The NASDAQ exchange is known for being the exchange where most technology companies are listed. Stocks that have four letters in their symbol are NASDAQ traded stocks. NASDAQ offers two types of listings: NASDAQ Small Cap and NASDAQ National Market System. Some quotation carriers add the symbols SC and NMS in their quote to indicate Small Cap (NASDAQ SC: XYZT) vs. National Market systems and (NASDAQ NM: XYZT)

NASDAQ Small Cap Market is a market for securities of smaller, less-capitalized companies (small caps) that do not qualify for inclusion in the NASDAQ National Market. Small cap companies range from a $250,000,000 to $1 billion capitalization.

NASDAQ is a computerized system established by the NASD to facilitate trading by providing broker/dealers with current bid and ask price quotes on over-the-counter stocks and some listed stocks. Unlike the AMEX and the NYSE, the NASDAQ (once an acronym for the National Association of Securities Dealers Automated Quotation system) does not have a physical trading floor that brings together buyers and sellers. Instead, all trading on the NASDAQ exchange is done over a network of computers and telephones. Also, the NASDAQ does not employ market specialists to buy unfilled orders, as the NYSE does. Orders for stock are sent out electronically on the NASDAQ, where market makers list their buy and sell prices. Once a price is agreed upon, the transaction is executed electronically.

In order to be eligible to list a company on the NASDAQ Small Cap you must meet the following criteria:

1. **Shareholders' equity of $5,000,000 (which is more than AMEX requires) or $50,000,000 market cap (which is less than AMEX requires)**
2. **$750,000 net income from continuing operations in the latest fiscal year and two out of the last three years**
3. **1,000,000 publicly held shares**
4. **Market value of public share $5,000,000**
5. **Minimum bid price $4**
6. **Shareholders 300 (less than AMEX and NYSE)**
7. **Operating history of one year or $50,000,000 market value of the listed securities**

In order to be eligible to list a company on the NASDAQ National Marketing Systems you must meet the following criteria:

1. **Shareholders equity of $15,000,000**

2. **$1,000,000 net income from continuing operations in the latest fiscal year and out of the last three years.**

3. **1,000,000 publicly held shares**

4. **Market value of public share $5,000,000**

5. **Minimum bid price $4**

6. **300 shareholders (less than AMEX and NYSE) and Operating history of one year or $50,000,000 market value of the listed securities.**

This is just a brief overview of the listing requirements for the NMS. For a complete list, go to our website www.BruceABerman.com.

OTC Bulletin Board

OTC Bulletin Board is an exchange owned by NASDAQ. More commonly it is known as the "Bulletin Board." The OTC listing requirements for companies stipulates substantially less capital, and, unlike NASDAQ, the minimum trading price of a company's stock is not an issue. In an attempt to provide investors as much information as possible, the OTC regulations have become stricter in the past few years.

OTC BB is a security, which is not traded on an exchange, usually due to an inability to meet listing requirements. For such securities, broker/dealers negotiate directly with one another over computer networks and by phone; their activities are monitored by the NASD. OTC stocks are usually very risky since they are the stocks that are not considered large or stable enough to trade on a major exchange. They also tend to trade infrequently, making the bid-ask spread larger.

The OTC BB is not an issuer listing service, market, or exchange. Although the OTC BB does not have any listing requirements per se, to be eligible for quotation on the OTC BB, issuers must remain current in their filings with the SEC or applicable regulatory authority. Market makers will not be permitted to begin quotation of a security whose issuer does not meet this filing requirement. Securities already quoted on the OTC BB that become delinquent in their required filings will be removed following a 30 or 60-day grace period if they do not make their required filing during that time. A fifth character of "E" in a security's trading symbol is used to denote securities that the NASD believes are delinquent in their required filings; securities so denoted will be removed from the OTC BB after the applicable grace period expires.

Pink Sheets

In the summer of 1999, the National Association of Securities Dealers (NASD) began the process of de-listing over 3,000 companies from the OTC Bulletin Board. This left many OTC stocks with virtually no visibility in the securities markets. In response, the Pink Sheets expanded its mission to provide a centralized source of quotations and information about OTC BB securities, by introducing its real-time Electronic Quotation Service for the OTC market in the fall of 1999.

The Pink Sheets' Electronic Quotation Service is a nexus in which competitive market makers display real-time prices and potential liquidity in thousands of domestic equities, Level I ADRs, and foreign ordinaries. Pink Sheets offer the same transparency and the same market makers as NASDAQ and the OTC Bulletin Board for companies that are unable or choose not to list their securities on NASDAQ or an exchange. It's that simple.

Available at no cost to issuers, the Electronic Quotation Service allows real-time quotations from competing OTC BB market makers, thus facilitating a transparent OTC BB market for your securities, and paving the way for a more efficient OTC BB marketplace.

Now investors can have access to accurate pricing, as well as current company information and news. As with the Electronic Quotation Service, there is no cost to issuers for this service.

While companies do not have to be Securities and Exchange Commission (SEC) reporting to be quoted on the Pink Sheets, it is highly recommended that issuers make available company information to shareholders and market participants in a timely manner.

How does my company become a Pink Sheets-quoted company?

Only SEC-registered broker/dealers (market makers) can quote securities in the Pink Sheets. Issuers may contact a registered broker/dealer for sponsorship of a security in the Pink Sheets. The market maker must then file a Form 211 with the NASD OTC Compliance Unit, along with two copies of the required issuer information. Pink Sheet quotes will be permitted after a successful review by the NASD.

Sarbanes-Oxley Act of 2002

The Sarbanes-Oxley Act of 2002, also know as the Corporate Responsibilities Act of 2002, was signed in July 2002, in the wake of the Enron and other accounting and corporate governance scandals. These company embarrassments motivated the federal government to introduce radical reforms in the four key areas below, imposing stricter regulations and duties for public companies.

Corporate responsibility

Requires CEOs and CFOs to certify financial reports and forfeit profits and bonuses from earnings restated due to securities fraud, puts restrictions on the time executives can sell their stock, prohibits company loans to executives, and requires immediate disclosure in "plain English" of material changes in a company's financial condition.

New Criminal Penalties

The new penalties created a 20-year prison term for destroying, altering, or fabricating records in federal investigations, or any "scheme or artifice" to defraud shareholders, raised maximum penalty for securities fraud to 25 years, increased CEO and CFO penalties for false statements to the SEC or failing to certify financial reports to a $5,000,000 fine, increased prison terms for all other types of securities fraud, and requires companies to hold key audit documents for five years and e-mails to five years.

Accounting Regulations

The new law calls for companies to establish a five-member oversight board with investigating and disciplinary powers. The board's members will serve on a full-time basis. No member may, concurrent with service on the board, "share in any of the profits of, or receive payments from, a public accounting firm," other than "fixed continuing payments," such as retirement payments. Members of the board are appointed by the commission, "after consultation with" the Chairman of the Federal Reserve Board and the Secretary of the Treasury.

The board duties are:

1. **Register public accounting firms;**

2. **Establish, or adopt, by rule, "auditing, quality control, ethics, independence, and other standards relating to the preparation of audit reports for issuers";**

3. **Conduct inspections of accounting firms;**

4. **Conduct investigations and disciplinary proceedings,**

and impose appropriate sanctions;

5. Perform such other duties or functions as necessary or appropriate;

6. Enforce compliance with the Act, the rules of the board, professional standards, and the securities laws relating to the preparation and issuance of audit reports and the obligations and liabilities of accountants with respect thereto;

7. Set the budget and manage the operations of the board and the staff of the board.

New Protections

Lengthening the statue of limitations on securities fraud to five years, or two from discovery, gives freedom of whistle-blowers to sue and prove retribution, forbids investment firms from retaliating against analysts who criticize a firm's clients, pays wronged investors with SEC imposed penalties, and prevents officials facing fraud judgments from taking refuge in bankruptcy.

Acquisitions Before and After Going Public

We are a private company. How can we acquire a company?

It is more common than you think for private companies to make corporate acquisitions. ***The most common ways are making acquisitions for stock, cash, and or seller financing.*** The first thing you need to know before making an acquisition is "Why is the seller selling?" Reasons like retirement, selling one business to start another, or a belief that selling to you is going to make the seller more money in the long run are good reasons. If the seller is selling because he can't make it, you need to look much harder at your potential acquisitions and make sure you don't get a pig in a poke.

Why are you interested in buying another company? The most common reasons are to secure a product or service you need, purchase a business in the same industry as yours to expand, and to shelve a competitor's product.

Private companies acquiring companies for stock

Hypothetically, take a company that owned many auto body shops; we will call them ABC Body Shops. They are doing what is called a "roll up." Their plan appears to be to acquire as many body shops in key locations as they can and acquire these small body shops using ABC Body Shop stock, which they are valuing between $3 and $15 per share, and to value at a price of three times earnings of the company they are acquiring. Then ABC Body Shops can put them all together, to either take them public (at a 20-30 times earnings basis), or sell the entire chain to a major insurance carrier to repair vehicles insured by the carrier at a reduced rate.

ABC Body Shops is a private company. They have raised money based on a valuation prepared by an independent party. This valuation values their stock today at $3 per share. ABC has a business plan showing that if it meets its projections, it should go public at $15 per share. Let's say it wants to buy a body shop that earns $250,000 a year. Based on the three times earnings basis, that makes the company they acquire worth $750,000 in stock. Now, do you value the stock at the $3 price they have been raising money at, or the $15 projected going public price?

Based on the above scenario, if I were selling my company, I would want 250,000 shares of the new company (using their $3 per share money raising valuation). ABC Body Shops would try to sell me on the $15 future price. I am not falling for that.

I know ABC is raising money at $3 per share and paying out about 13% in commissions, so, if they were to buy my company for cash ($750,000), they would have to sell almost 300,000 shares at $3 per share, and after commissions, they would have $750,000 in cash.

Why am I willing to sell for all stock? Because I believe they are going to go public and my shares will be worth

Company Stock Valued at $750,000	Their Method	Berman Differential Method	Berman Differential Added Value*
Selling Price	$15 per Share	$3 per Share	
# of Shares	50,000	250,000	
Value of Shares After Going Public at $15 per share	$750,000	$3,750,000	$3,000,000*

* The Berman Differential Added Value is the potential Dollar-Value-Difference of doing business one-way over another

far more than the $3 per share price; maybe as high as $15 a share if everything goes right.

It only makes sense to buy or sell a company for stock when the surviving company intends to go public. Owning a minority stake in a private company doesn't do much for you.

Private companies acquiring companies for cash

You agree on a price and you pay for the company in cash, right? Unfortunately it's not that easy. Many business owners have acquired companies for cash and feel they don't have to plan for anything else. If you are buying a company for cash, ***make sure you have ample cash reserves,*** not only to get your business through a potential slump but the business of the company you acquired.

Companies usually have skeletons in their closets that take time to uncover. Think about your business. Last year did you write something off on your taxes that might not pass an audit? Did you have a dissatisfied customer who may file a lawsuit? Sell any products that might be returned? Sell any products that might break or need a warranty? Or, maybe you sold a product that a year from now has to be recalled. So the rule of thumb, when you acquire a company in a similar industry, is to assume they have three times as many skeletons in their closet as you do.

Private companies acquiring for seller financing

This is the best way to go. Say I am a private company and am going to buy a company on a note basis. *My gut tells me if any skeletons come up in the company I acquire, I can just offset their note and deduct the costs of any skeletons from what I owe them.* Well, this thought process once cost me millions of dollars, and hopefully you will benefit from my lesson. I know I have.

I believe the best advice I can give someone is from my business dealings that didn't go as planned.

My company acquired our main supplier. We purchased the company for about $500,000 cash and a $2,000,000 note. Several months after we acquired this company, we began to uncover a can of worms. They had a design defect in their product that we could not fix, their prior customers wanted to sue them (now us), and the organization was in chaos.

A few months into it, we ascertained that our potential liabilities from making this acquisition were going to far exceed the $2,000,000 we owed and we made this no secret to the people from which we bought the company. We started to send letters documenting our damages, asking them to respond with a solution.

They responded with a solution, all right. In the height of our season, when we were sitting on about $6,000,000 in cash in four different banks, they filed a lawsuit against us for an "anticipatory breach of contract." This meant our note was not due now, but they believed that, when it was due (in a few months), we would not pay; therefore, they sued us now. *They were actually* *successful in convincing a judge, without notice to us, to give them a pre-judgment writ of attachment for $2,000,000.*

We never kept more than $1,500,000 in any individual bank (for fear of a bank failure). They went to each of our banks and filed their $2,000,000 writ of attachment. All four of our banks had about $1.5 million. What happened was all four of our banks froze our accounts and all $6,000,000 of our operating cash was frozen. We offered to take $2,000,000 and set it in a trust account, but their attorney stalled. Knowing he had frozen all of our cash, he was going to wait us out. Knowing that with all of our cash frozen in the height of our season, the only way we could free up our cash was to pay him off, and he wouldn't take a settlement unless we agreed to pay him the $2,000,000 and agree not to sue his clients. We had a business decision to make, and we decided to pay the $2,000,000.

So, lesson learned. Just because you buy a business on a note, don't think the note gives you the right to offset the note holder for their wrongdoings. Most notes have to be paid with no right of offset, and your only recourse is to pay the note in full and then sue the seller. When you buy a business, if you buy it on a contract, you may be in a better position than if you sign a note. I will never sign a note to buy a another business again.

Public companies acquiring businesses

Public companies follow the same purchasing options private firms do in acquiring companies for stock, cash, seller financing, or a combination of any of the aforementioned. Most of the time you will see acquisitions by public companies using their stock as currency.

Why do public companies want to buy private companies?
There are many different reasons, and if you are selling your

company to a public company, the sooner you figure out why they are buying, the better. The typical reasons are: expanding their business, shelving a competitor's product, the company to be acquired has cash reserves or a desirable revenue stream, or the public company wants some of the assets of the private company (real estate, leases, etc.). The good news is if a public company is trying to acquire your business, you can look at the public company's press release SEC filings, and any other publicly released information for clues on why they are pursuing you.

Believe it or not, public companies do not always tell you the real reason why they are interested in acquiring your company out of fear you will want a higher price for your business. What do you do when a public company is interested in acquiring your firm?

1. Find out why they are interested.

2. What might not be valuable to you may be valuable to the public company. Once you figure out why and what they are interested in, you can negotiate a more favorable price.

3. Evaluate how you are to be compensated: stock, cash, or note. Which gives you what you are looking for in life?

4. Meet with a Certified Public Accountant and analyze the tax consequences of the proposed transaction.

5. ***If you are to receive stock for your company, there are two major concerns you will have; the valuation of both the acquirer and the acquired and most importantly, the restrictions on selling the stock you receive.*** In order for you to sell the stock you are to receive for your company, it will have to be registered to become free trading. This can be a costly and/or a time-consuming process. Make sure to consult a securities attorney on documenting this transaction and get a written explanation and agreement regarding when and how you can register your stock. There are also

restrictions on how much stock a shareholder may sell in any given three-month period. Make sure that you are able to sell what you want when you want.

6. **Cash is cash**. You know exactly how much you are getting and how much tax you have to pay. A public company will usually be more generous in a purchase of a company when the purchase is for stock. Sometimes the price can be twice as much for a company paid in stock than in cash. So, evaluate this transaction carefully.

7. **Liquidity in the public company's stock.** Just because a company is public doesn't mean the stock you get (once registered for sale) is readily marketable. Some public companies do not have enough daily activity trading in their stock to handle a large seller. A good rule of thumb is to look at the average daily trading volume of the public company and figure that you can probably sell 1% of the daily trading average without causing the price of the stock to plummet. Example: company XYZ trades 500,000 shares a day. If you calculate 1% would equal 5,000 shares you might be able to sell without affecting the price of the company's stock. Now, if you were to receive 1,000,000 shares of stock for your company, and the average trading was 500,000 a day, it would take you 200 trading days to sell off the stock. You need to carefully examine how much stock you desire to sell, in any given time, vs. how much the market can bear. If you tried to sell 100,000 shares a day in a company that usually trades 500,000 shares a day, the price of the stock would most likely plummet, giving you less of a reward for selling your company.

8. **Review the stock exchange where the public company is listed.** For example, NYSE and NASDAQ, National Marketing Systems, maintain more stringent requirements for companies to be listed than the AMEX and NASDAQ Small Cap. The OTC BB is known as the "Wild West" and has a higher failure rate of public companies than any other

exchange. If I had a technology company, I would prefer it to be listed on NASDAQ. Other than technology, my next choice would be the NYSE.

9. **Are you selling a pig in a poke?** Now, if your company is being overvalued or has problems you know about and they don't, and a public company wants to buy you, it better be for cash. If you were capable of selling a lemon to them, just imagine how many other problem companies they have bought from people who wanted to cash out quickly.

10. **Does a reputable accounting firm audit the company? What disclosures do the accountants make?** Most novices, when they read or review financial statements, skip right to the numbers and don't read the disclosures made by the accountants. There can be disclaimers in the footnotes that would seriously impact the business in the near future and they need to be reviewed and analyzed in a non-cash transaction.

Bankrupt Not Broke: Bankruptcy as a tool

Bankruptcy has gone in and out of fashion more times than my grandmother's clothes. In the early 1980s, if either you personally or your business went bankrupt, you were like someone with leprosy. Then, in the late 1980s, everyone was doing it. The technology boom of the 90s ended the popularity of bankruptcy, but then it fell back in favor in the late 90s and early 2000s when dot com became dot bomb and bankruptcies were on the rise again. How often do you open a newspaper and read about Fortune 500 companies in the airlines, telecom, technology, or even large retail chains that have been in business for years, going in and out of bankruptcy or threatening bankruptcy?

Why are these companies going bankrupt or threatening bankruptcy? The average person thinks the simple answer is they're out of money. Wrong. ***Companies use bankruptcy as a***

negotiating ploy all the time. Just the threat of filing bankruptcy can save companies millions of dollars in contract negotiating. Large corporations use it as a tool when negotiating with their unions. So what does that have to do with me, the little guy? Everything, if you know how to use it as a tool. Here is a news article on American Airlines.

Following is an excerpt from a press release published on April, 2003, regarding American Airlines:

> **American Warns of Bankruptcy Filing**
>
> **American Airlines said it would file for bankruptcy protection Tuesday if a group of pilots is able to delay a union's vote on part of a $1.8-billion labor-savings plan.**
>
> *The pilots want voting on the $660-million agreement suspended, pilots' spokesman Sam Mayer said. The vote shouldn't happen until negotiations with American, the world's biggest carrier, are completed and the full plan is reviewed, he said.*
>
> *The deadline for voting, which began April 1, is Monday.*
>
> **"If we don't have ratification by all unions Tuesday morning, we will file bankruptcy,"** *said Bruce Hicks, an American spokesman.*

The big guys use bankruptcy and the threat of bankruptcy as a tool and so can you. The threat of bankruptcy can give you the leverage to renegotiate contracts and other obligations. Here are some typical examples of using the threat of bankruptcy to renegotiate your debts. Keep in mind, if you threaten bankruptcy you better be prepared to file It's not a threat to be made without careful review and discussions with bankruptcy counsel. Once you release a letter that says you are insolvent, three of your creditors can legally get together and force you into involuntary bankruptcy, if they desire.

In all dealings with creditors, with whom you are delinquent, it is paramount that you deal with them in a calm, humble manner. Anything short of that is likely to be met with a "no." If you approach a business creditor (in most cases) and calmly and humbly admit you have problems, let him know you want to work it out, and offer a possible solution, you are more likely to get an agreement than if you try and bully him into one.

Situation 1. You want to stay in business but you need your supplier to keep supplying your product, even though you are delinquent on your payable of $100,000.

A. You need them to continue to supply more products so that you can stay in business, even though you can't pay your delinquent bill at the moment.

B. You will pay C.O.D. for all the goods shipped to you going forward.

C. In 60 days you will pay C.O.D. for the goods, plus $5,000 a month toward the old bill.

D. Very humbly inform them, that if you can't get them to work along these lines you *may* have to file bankruptcy.

E. You have reviewed your company's financial position with an attorney, and he believes if you file bankruptcy, after legal fees and liquidation costs, the creditors would be left with about $0.10 on the dollar (if that happens to be true).

Situation 2. You do not need any of your suppliers, you can get new ones, but you can't pay your debts at their current payment schedule and stay in business.

A. Inform them that your cash flow will not allow you to pay all your debts and you have two choices: either file bankruptcy or work out a repayment plan for all your creditors.

B. You can pay 100% of their debt, but you need to restructure the debt, lengthen the term, and cut the monthly payment amount.

C. If they won't do the above, you may have to file bankruptcy.

Situation 3. You have some cash and want to settle all your debts for a percentage of what you owe them.

A. Inform them you have X amount of dollars and if they agree to a one-time pay off of 50 cents on the dollar, you can pay all your creditors and go forward in business.

B. If they won't accept a discount, you will have to file bankruptcy, and you believe the legal fees will reduce the number they will ultimately get, whenever the bankruptcy is resolved. That could be as short as a few months or over a year.

Actually filing personal bankruptcy and keeping your money

I walked away from potential liabilities of over $100,000,000 using "bankruptcy as a tool" and left the bankruptcy court with almost $2,000,000 in my pockets. I also settled a $22,000,000 IRS claim in bankruptcy court for 1-1/2 cents on the dollar.

Here is how I did it. Back in the late 80s, a company I owned was being sued because a product we bought from someone else malfunctioned. We were the ones with *deep pockets* so everyone sued us. After spending millions of dollars in legal fees, it was time for a new strategy. The harder I fought to bring it to a resolution, the more I saw that the attorneys had little motivation to resolve the case. After all, the longer it went on, the more money they made. None were working on a contingency basis.

At this time I moved to Texas. I moved there for a variety of reasons. Once in Texas, I learned about what is called a *homestead.* Apparently, at the time, Texas and Florida have what is known as "an unlimited homestead exemption" if you go bankrupt. What that means is this: if you are a Texas resident (at the time the requirement was six months) and you owned a home on less than five acres in a city or 100 acres in a rural area, and you subsequently went bankrupt, you could keep all the equity in your home, even if you discharged your debts in bankruptcy.

I realized that the cost of fighting the lawsuit was most likely going to eat up all my capital, as well as stop me from pursuing any productive ventures while I waited for a resolution. I decided it was time to go forward with a Chapter 11 Bankruptcy. At the time, I owned a newly constructed palatial home of approximately 10,000 square feet on 98 acres of land. It was called White Oaks Ranch and was designed to look like Tara, Scarlett O'Hara's home in Gone with the Wind.

Without going through all the boring details, here is what happened. My potential creditors were very upset. They implied that while I was living in California, I ran a business in California, I got into $100,000,000 in legal battles in California, and I purposely took all my available cash and spent it on a $2,000,000 home for the sole purpose of filing bankruptcy and dismissing their lawsuits and keeping the equity in my home. Well, the judge said something to this effect: ***"Even if Mr. Berman did what is being alleged, which he is disputing, it is perfectly legal to move from California to Texas and file bankruptcy to avoid creditors. Case dismissed." He dismissed $100,000,000 in potential liabilities and let me keep my $2,000,000 home.***

This is a picture of the $2,000,000, 100 acre ranch I bought and kept after walking out of bankruptcy court at age 30.

Basically, Florida and Texas allow you to keep your home, regardless of its value, in bankruptcy. Recently there have been some billion-dollar corporate bankruptcies where the corporate executives from those companies owned $10,000,000 and $20,000,000 estates in Texas and Florida, sparking discussion in Congress about closing the homestead loophole. Some of the advocates of this law want to change the amount of time you must live in a state before you are considered a resident; others want to limit the dollar amount of the property, and there are some that want to do away with it entirely. It is impossible to know what the future holds, but my guess is if this century-old loophole is changed, the part of the law that will change is the amount of time one must reside in Texas or Florida before you are protected. I suggest contacting a bankruptcy attorney in your area and find out how this may apply to you.

Bankruptcy and the IRS

IRS offices and agents can be intimidating and the agents know this. IRS agents are comfortable doing battle in their office, under their rules. Think about it. All day long they file the same type of forms, liens, collection notices, and lawsuits in the same manner. They seem to have an unlimited budget to pursue a claim. It makes total sense to them to spend thousands of dollars to collect a claim that may only be a thousand dollars. After all, it's not their money they're spending. It's the American taxpayers.

Bankruptcy court is known as "a court of equities." What does that mean? Well, the simplest explanation is it is a place to resolve legal disputes in the most efficient time and cost-effective manner.

Bankruptcy judges are very strict on things like excessive attorneys fees, dragging out the litigation process, and lengthy court hearings.

Form **6338(C)** (Rev. June 1986)	Department of the Treasury – Internal Revenue Service **Proof of Claim for Internal Revenue Taxes** (Bankruptcy Code Cases)	Case Number ▮▮▮

Type of Bankruptcy Case: Chap. 11

Date of Petition: ▮▮▮

United States Bankruptcy Court for the __EASTERN__ District of __TEXAS__
SHERMAN DIVISION

In the Matter of:

Bruce A. Berman
P. O. Box ▮▮▮
Pilot Point, TX 76250

Taxpayer Identifying Number
Social Security Number: ▮▮▮
Employer Identification Number

AMENDMENT NO. 2 TO PROOF OF CLAIM DATED 07-23-90

1. The undersigned, whose business address is __1100 Commerce St., Code 5027 DAL, Dallas, TX 75242__, is the agent of the Department of Treasury, Internal Revenue Service, and is authorized to make full proof of claim on behalf of the United States.
2. The debtor is indebted to the United States in the sum of **$21,951,868.25** as of the petition date.
3. The amount of all payments on this claim has been credited and deducted for the purpose of making this claim.
4. The ground of liability is taxes due under the internal revenue laws of the United States.

A. Secured Claims (Notice of Federal tax lien filed under internal revenue laws before petition date)

Kind of Tax	Tax Period	Date Tax Assessed	Tax Due	Penalty to Petition Date	Interest to Petition Date	Notice of Tax Lien Filed: Date	Office Location
			$	$			

For the purposes of section 506(b) of the Bankruptcy Code, post petition interest may be payable.

B. Unsecured Priority Claims under section 507(a)(6) of the Bankruptcy Code

Kind of Tax	Tax Period	Date Tax Assessed	Tax Due	Interest to Petition Date
			$	$

TOTAL UNSECURED PRIORITY CLAIMS ITEMIZED ON ATTACHED SCHEDULE B

C. Unsecured General Claims

Kind of Tax	Tax Period	Date Tax Assessed	Tax Due	Interest to Petition Date
			$	$

Penalty to date of petition on unsecured priority claims . . . . $ 612,842.25
Penalty to date of petition on unsecured general claims . . . . $ .00
No note or other negotiable instrument has been received for the account or any part of it, except NONE
No judgment has been rendered on this claim, except NONE
This claim is not subject to any setoff or counterclaim, except NONE
No security interest is held, except for the secured claims listed in item 4A above and NONE
To the extent that post petition penalties and interest are nondischargeable and remain unpaid, they may be collectible from the debtor.

Penalty for Presenting Fraudulent Claim – Fine of not more than $5,000 or imprisonment for not more than 5 years or both – Title 18 U.S.C. Section 152.

Signature: ▮▮▮
Title: Advisor, Insolvency Section
Date: ▮▮▮
Telephone Number: ▮▮▮

Part 3 - For Fiduciary (or Court, if Part 1 is sent to Fiduciary)
Form 6338(C) (Rev. 6-86)

In 1989 the IRS sued me for approximately $22,000,000. They wanted to overturn a tax shelter in which I had invested. They seemed to have an unlimited amount of resources with which to attack me. I believe the main reason they pursued me so relentlessly was because I was in the business of selling tax shelters, making me a competitor in their eyes, taking cash from them and giving it to my clients and myself.

I'll never forget the day I met with the IRS in their offices in Laguna Niguel to discuss the case. It was the first day of the first Persian Gulf War, when the US was dropping bombs on Baghdad. I met with the head counsel and a few of his assistants. The government had told its employees that it was their option to stay or leave because of the potential of terrorism, and it appeared as though the building had been 99% evacuated. The IRS agent asked me if I wanted to reschedule the appointment, and I responded, "I am sure the last place a terrorist is going to attack would be the IRS. That would cause the average American to rejoice. Let's have the meeting."

The meeting didn't go well. The IRS started out saying they heard that my business partner actually faked his own death and was living somewhere in Mexico. Since he was my closest friend, this statement not only brought up horrendous feelings, it angered me. By my reaction, the IRS agents could tell they hit a sore spot and we moved on.

During this meeting they explained that even though they were suing me for $22,000,000, they thought I only owed $11,000,000. They weren't sure what year it would have been due, so they put $11,000,000 due for two separate years as a legal tactic. The judge hated this maneuver in bankruptcy court. It basically made them look like liars and bullies. We couldn't reach an agreement, but it was nice to know it was now just $11,000,000.

Well, since I had entered a Chapter 11 Bankruptcy in Texas, the IRS agents had to come from their comfortable post in Laguna Niguel, California to Tyler, Texas for the trial. They lost the home court advantage. Now, the first thing the judge did was ask them to explain how I owed them $22,000,000. They explained that they just filed it for $22,000,000 and it was really $11,000,000. Like I said, strike 1 for their credibility with the judge.

The IRS tactics seemed to be to try to drag everything out and wear me down in legal motions and costs. Well, my side came to the Tyler court for trial and the IRS apparently came prepared to stall. It was amazing, as much as they acted as though they wanted to take me to trial, the less they appeared to have actually prepared for it.

The judge ordered the case to proceed. The IRS was claiming that several years earlier I had taken a $4,000,000 deduction, which I did, for my purchase of 40 windmills. They alleged that I didn't pass the test for the deduction. The judge jumped in and asked how a $4,000,000 deduction could create an $11,000,000 tax burden. The IRS tried to explain interest and penalties but they looked like even bigger liars in the judge's eyes. Remember, their tactics tend to intimidate you with big numbers and paperwork. I don't know about you, but the day I got the $22,000,000 tax claim from them, I was intimidated, but I was not going to be bullied. I had them in my backyard and I was prepared.

The IRS started with their case. Here were their points:

1. I paid too much for the windmills; therefore, the claim shouldn't be allowed.

2. I wasn't in the business for a profit; it was a passive investment.

3. They weren't installed by the end of the year.

4. I wasn't at risk because I bought them on a note from my own company.

Well, that was their case. Here is what we did:

1. Provided data that, yes, my company sold windmills to investors at $220,000. The actual cost I paid was $100,000 each; therefore, I did not overpay.

2. My tax returns showed several million dollars in income (or else why would I need the deduction?) all from the energy business so you couldn't call it a passive investment.

3. I had a picture of me holding a newspaper marked December 28 next to the windmills, showing they were installed on time.

4. This was the best: I don't recommend you do this, but I couldn't resist. I got up from my chair on the stand and walked out to the front of the courtroom and then walked back and sat in my chair on the stand. The IRS agent (who, along with everyone else was stunned), and asked me what I thought I was doing. Well, I told him, "You have been arguing for an hour that I wasn't at risk when I bought those 40 windmills, so I shouldn't get my deduction. I just had to go out and look at the front door to see if it still said United States Bankruptcy Court, because I could swear, when I woke up this morning, I was supposed to be in bankruptcy court all because of the windmill business and my purchase of those 40 windmills. Now, if ending up in bankruptcy court isn't 'at risk' what is? Dying like my partner?"

That shook them all up. We went into a recess and my lawyer said, "Let's make them an offer. They are ready to settle." I wasn't nervous about the $22,000,000 claim, but I was nervous about $1,000,000 in other possible deductions so I agreed to give them a face-saving offer of 1-1/2 cents on the dollar. Not in cash, mind you. They don't need the cash. I agreed to give them a lien against my house with no interest or payments, all due whenever I sold my house. They accepted. You have to let people save face in business or there is no reason for them to settle. The funny thing is, I sold that house two years later and the IRS forgot to file their lien. It was tempting not to let them know, but I did the right thing and sent them their money. It was funny calling up the agent, telling him his mistake, and asking where he wanted the check sent.

```
                              INITIAL COPY

                      UNITED STATES TAX COURT


        BRUCE A. BERMAN,                    )
                                            )
                    Petitioner,             )
                                            )        Docket No. ███████
                v.                          )
                                            )
        COMMISSIONER OF INTERNAL REVENUE,   )
                                            )
                    Respondent.             )
        _____)


                    STIPULATION OF THE PARTIES
              WHEREAS the parties have settled this case and,
        simultaneously with the filing of this stipulation, are filing
        a decision document; and
              WHEREAS the purpose of this stipulation is to set
        forth the terms of the settlement into which the parties have
        entered; and
              WHEREAS this stipulation will be filed with the United
        States Tax Court in the above-captioned case and in the United
        States Bankruptcy Court for the Eastern District of Texas in
        the case entitled In re Bruce A. Berman, Debtor, Chapter 11
        Case No. ███████ ("bankruptcy proceeding"); NOW THEREFORE, it
        is hereby
              1.  STIPULATED AND AGREED that the federal tax
        liability of petitioner is $300,000. It is further
```

Bankruptcy in general

Enough of my stories. Here is some more information about different types of bankruptcies and their rules. What is bankruptcy? It's a proceeding in federal court in which an insolvent debtor's assets are liquidated and the debtor is relieved of further liability. Chapter 7 of the Bankruptcy Reform Act deals with liquidation, while Chapter 11 deals with reorganization.

What exactly is bankruptcy?

Bankruptcy is a federal court process designed to help consumers and businesses eliminate their debts or repay them under the protection of the bankruptcy court.

Aren't there different kinds of bankruptcy?

Yes. Bankruptcies can generally be described as ***"liquidation"*** or ***"reorganization."***

Liquidation Bankruptcy is called Chapter 7. Under Chapter 7 Bankruptcy, a consumer or business asks the bankruptcy court to wipe out (discharge) the debts owed. Certain debts cannot be discharged, which are discussed below. In exchange for the discharge of debts, the business's assets or the consumer's non-exempt property is sold (or "liquidated"), and the proceeds used to pay off creditors. The property a consumer might lose is discussed below.

There are several types of reorganization bankruptcy. Consumers with secured debts under $871,550 and unsecured debts under $269,250 can file for Chapter 13. Family farmers can file for Chapter 12. Consumers with debts in excess of the Chapter 13 debt limits or businesses can file for Chapter 11, a complex, time-consuming and expensive process. In any reorganization bankruptcy, you file a plan with the bankruptcy court proposing how you will repay your creditors. Some debts must be repaid in full, others you need pay only a percentage, and some aren't paid at all. Some debts you have to pay with interest, some are paid at the beginning of your plan and some at the end.

Chapter 7

Chapter 7 Bankruptcy is the part of the U.S. Bankruptcy Code describing the liquidation of the assets and the elimination of debts for a consumer or company after bankruptcy.

Involuntary Chapter 7

Involuntary Chapter 7 Bankruptcy is when a group of creditors (people owed money by the same person or corporation), file a petition to force an individual or corporation into Chapter 7 bankruptcy.

Chapter 10

Chapter 11 Bankruptcy is the part of the U.S. Bankruptcy Code describing how a company can file for court protection. Reorganization occurs under an independent, court-appointed manager.

Chapter 11

Chapter 11 Bankruptcy is the part of the U.S. Bankruptcy Code describing how a company or individual debtor can file for court protection. In the case of a corporation, reorganization occurs under the existing management.

Chapter 13

Chapter 13 Bankruptcy is the part of the U.S. Bankruptcy Code allowing an individual to begin debt repayment without forfeiting property. Chapter 13 requires that the debtor maintain a source of income and adhere to a payment schedule set forth by the court.

What generally happens in consumer bankruptcy cases?

In a **Chapter 7** case, you file several forms with the bankruptcy court listing income and expenses, assets, debts, and property transactions for the past two years. The cost to file is $200, which may be waived for people who receive public assistance or live below the poverty level. A court-appointed person, the trustee, is assigned to oversee your case. About a month after filing, you must attend a "meeting of creditors" where the trustee reviews your forms and asks any questions. Despite the name, creditors rarely attend. If you have any non-exempt property, you must give it (or its value in cash) to the trustee. The meeting lasts about five minutes. Three to six months later, you receive a notice from the court that "all debts that qualified for discharge were discharged." Then your case is over.

Chapter 13 is a little different. You file the same forms plus a proposed repayment plan, in which you describe how you intend to repay your debts over the next three or, in some cases, five years. The cost to file is $185 (it cannot be waived), and a trustee is assigned to oversee the case. Here, too, you attend the creditors' meeting. Often one or two creditors attend this meeting, especially if they don't like something in your plan. After the meeting of the creditors, you attend a hearing before a bankruptcy judge who either confirms or denies your plan. If your plan is confirmed, and you make all the payments called for under your plan, you often receive a discharge of any balance owed at the end of your case.

Non-dischargeable Debts

The following debts are non-dischargeable in both Chapter 7 and Chapter 13. If you file for Chapter 7, these will remain when your case is over. If you file for Chapter 13, these debts will have to be paid in full during your plan. If they are not, the balance will remain at the end of your case:

- **Debts you forget to list in your bankruptcy papers, unless the creditor learns of your bankruptcy case**

- **Child support and alimony**

- **Debts for personal injury or death caused by your intoxicated driving**

- **Student loans, unless it would be an undue hardship for you to repay**

- **Fines and penalties imposed for violating the law, such** as traffic tickets and criminal restitution, and

- **Recent income tax debts and all other tax debts.**

In addition, the following debts may be declared non-dischargeable by a bankruptcy judge in Chapter 7 if the creditor challenges your request to discharge them. These debts may be discharged in Chapter 13. You can include them in your plan, and at the end of your case, the balance is wiped out:

- **Debts you incurred on the basis of fraud, such as lying on a credit application**

- **Credit purchases of $1,150 or more for luxury goods or services made within 60 days of filing**

- **Loans or cash advances of $1,150 or more taken within 60 days of filing**

- **Debts from willful or malicious injury to another person or another person's property**

- **Debts from embezzlement, larceny or breach of trust, and**

- **Debts you owe under a divorce decree or settlement unless, after bankruptcy you would still not be able to afford to pay them or the benefit you'd receive by the discharge outweighs any detriment to your ex-spouse (who would have to pay them if you discharge them in bankruptcy).**

What property might I lose if I file for bankruptcy?

You lose no property in Chapter 13. In Chapter 7, you select property you are eligible to keep from either a list of state exemptions or exemptions provided in the federal Bankruptcy Code. Most debtors use the exemptions provided by their state.

Exemptions are generally as follows:

- **Equity in your home, called a homestead exemption.** Under the Bankruptcy Code, you can exempt up to $17,425 of equity. Some states have no homestead exemption; others allow debtors to protect all or most of the equity in their home.

- **Insurance.** You usually get to keep the cash value of your policies.

- **Retirement plans.** Pensions, which qualify under the Employee Retirement Income Security Act (ERISA), are fully protected in bankruptcy. So are many other retirement benefits; often, however, IRAs and Keoghs are not.

- **Personal property.** You'll be able to keep most household goods, furniture, furnishings, clothing (other than furs), appliances, books and musical instruments. You may be limited up to $1,000 or so in how much jewelry you can keep. Most states let you keep a vehicle with no more than $2,400 of equity. And many states give you a "wild card" amount of money—often $1,000 or more—that you can apply toward any property.

- **Public benefits.** All public benefits, such as welfare, Social Security and unemployment insurance, are fully protected.

- **Tools used on your job.** You'll probably be able to keep up to a few thousand dollars worth of the tools used in your trade or profession.

- **Wages.** In most states, you can protect at least 75% of earned but unpaid wages.

Will I lose my house or apartment?

One of the biggest worries you may face when considering filing for bankruptcy is the possible loss of your home. Though there are a few situations where you may lose your home, keep in mind that bankruptcy is not designed to put you out on the street.

Home Ownership and Bankruptcy. If you are behind on your mortgage payments, you will almost certainly lose your house if you file a Chapter 7 Bankruptcy. Your mortgage lender will ask the bankruptcy court to lift the automatic stay to begin or resume foreclosure proceedings. In a Chapter 13 Bankruptcy, you will not lose your house if you immediately resume making regular payments called for under your agreement and repay your missed mortgage payments through your plan.

If you are current on your mortgage payments, you will not lose your house if you file for Chapter 13 Bankruptcy, as long as you continue to make your mortgage payments. In Chapter 7 Bankruptcy, whether or not you will lose your house depends on the amount of equity you have in the property and the amount of any homestead exemption (which varies state-to-state) to which you are entitled.

If the total amount of debt against your house is less than the market value, you may lose your house unless a homestead exemption entitles you to all or most of the equity

Renting and Bankruptcy. If you are current on your rent payments and file for bankruptcy, it's unlikely your landlord would ever find out. But if you are behind on your rent, there's a good chance that your landlord will begin eviction proceedings to get you out. Your inclination may be to file for bankruptcy just to get the automatic stay in place to stop the eviction. This will work, but not for very long. Expect your landlord to come into court to have the stay lifted, which is likely to be granted.

Why choose Chapter 13 over Chapter 7 Bankruptcy?

Although the overwhelming numbers of people who file for bankruptcy choose Chapter 7, there are several reasons why people select Chapter 13:

- You cannot file for Chapter 7 Bankruptcy if you received a Chapter 7 or Chapter 13 discharge within the previous six years (unless you paid off at least 70% of your unsecured debts in a Chapter 13 Bankruptcy). On the other hand, you can file for Chapter 13 Bankruptcy at any time.

- You have valuable non-exempt property

- You're behind on your mortgage or car loan. In Chapter 7, you'll have to give up the property or pay for it in full during your bankruptcy case. In Chapter 13, you can repay the arrears through your plan, and keep the property by making the payments required under the contract.

- You have debts that cannot be discharged in Chapter 7.

- You have co-debtors on personal (non-business) loans. In Chapter 7, the creditors will go after your co-debtors for payment. In Chapter 13, the creditors may not seek payment from your co-debtors for the duration of your case.

- You feel a moral obligation to repay your debts, you want to learn money management, or you hope new creditors might be more inclined to grant you credit after a Chapter 13 than they would after a Chapter 7.

An Overview of Chapter 7 Bankruptcy

Chapter 7 Bankruptcy refers to the chapter of the federal statutes (the Bankruptcy Code) that contains the bankruptcy law. Chapter 7 Bankruptcy is sometimes called "straight" bankruptcy. This bankruptcy cancels most of your debts; in exchange, you might have to surrender some of your property.

The whole Chapter 7 Bankruptcy process takes about four to six months, costs $200 in filing and administrative fees, and commonly requires only one trip to the courthouse.

To file for bankruptcy, you fill out a two-page petition and several other forms. Then you file the petition and forms with the bankruptcy court in your area. Basically, the forms ask you to describe:

- Your property
- Your current income and its sources
- Your current monthly living expenses
- Your debts
- Property you claim the law allows you to keep through the bankruptcy process (exempt property—most states let you keep clothing, household furnishings, Social Security payments you haven't spent and other basic items)
- Property you owned and money you spent during the previous two years, and
- Property you sold or gave away during the previous two years.

Filing for bankruptcy puts into effect something called the "automatic stay." The automatic stay immediately stops your creditors from trying to collect what you owe them. So, at least temporarily, creditors cannot legally grab (garnish) your wages, empty your bank account, go after your car, house or other property, or cut off your utility service or welfare benefits.

Until your bankruptcy case ends, your financial problems are in the hands of the bankruptcy court. It assumes legal control of the property you own (except your exempt property, which is yours to keep) and the debts you owe as of the date you file. Nothing can be sold or paid without the court's consent. You have control, with a few exceptions, of property and income you acquire after you file for bankruptcy.

The court exercises its control through a court-appointed person called a "bankruptcy trustee." The trustee is mostly interested in what you own and what property you claim as exempt. This is because the trustee's primary duty is to see that your creditors are paid as much as possible on what you owe them. And the more assets the trustee recovers for creditors, the more the trustee is paid.

The trustee goes through the papers you file and asks you questions at a short hearing, called the "creditors' meeting," which you must attend. This meeting is not likely to last more than five minutes. Creditors may attend, too, but rarely do.

After this meeting, the trustee collects the property that can be taken from you (your non-exempt property) to be sold to pay your creditors. You can surrender the property to the trustee, pay the trustee its fair market value or, if the trustee agrees, swap some exempt property of equal value for the non-exempt property. If the property isn't worth very much or would be cumbersome for the trustee to sell, the trustee can "abandon" the property—which means that you get to keep it. Very few people actually lose property in bankruptcy.

If you've pledged property as collateral for a loan, the loan is called a secured debt. The most common examples of collateral are houses and motor vehicles. In most cases, you'll either have to surrender the collateral to the creditor or make arrangements to pay for it during or after bankruptcy. If a creditor has recorded a lien against your property, that debt is also secured. You may be able to wipe out the lien in bankruptcy.

If, after you file for bankruptcy, you change your mind, you can ask the court to dismiss your case. As a general rule, a court will dismiss a Chapter 7 Bankruptcy case as long as the dismissal won't harm the creditors. Usually, you can file again if you want to, although you may have to wait 180 days.

At the end of the bankruptcy process, most of your debts are wiped out (discharged) by the court. You no longer legally owe your creditors. You can't file for Chapter 7 Bankruptcy again for another six years from the date of your filing.

Asset protection

It's not what you make. It's what you keep

I wish I had every dollar I made, but I don't. Sometimes I had to learn things the hard way. As I have said over and over in this book, I learned more from the business dealings that don't go as planned than I learned from the winners. The trick is not to make the same error in judgment twice. If you do make the same error twice, you get an "F" in my Master's Course in Becoming a Millionaire.

Protecting your assets? Let's start with the one closest to you. Are you married or thinking about getting married? Pre- and post-marital agreements will protect you, right? Wrong. They are a good start but they do have their ups and downs.

The Premarital Agreements

Here's an example of how pre-marital agreements fail to protect you. A wife signed a pre-marital agreement with her husband but still got more than outlined in the agreement. The wife had no assets going into the marriage but the husband had a million-dollar business. The husband went to a top family lawyer in his area to draw up what he felt was a solid premarital agreement.

Four years later the marriage ended with the wife filing for divorce. The husband's business had grown, however such growth was covered in the premarital agreement. Coincidentally, the husband was in a vicious lawsuit with a competitor over who had rights to a specific product.

The wife's lawyer informed her that based on the premarital

agreement she had signed, she wouldn't be entitled to very much in court. The wife was familiar with her husband's business and told her husband that she was going to go to his competitor and sign an affidavit telling them anything he needed her to say, which would help the competitor's lawsuit and devastate the husband.

Even though the wife may not have had any damaging information about the husband's business, he felt that her testimony to the competitor could cost him his business. The husband decided to give his wife a substantial sum of money.

So you see, there is no agreement that can protect you against every day events. Here the husband possessed what he thought was a bulletproof premarital agreement and the wife was able to take advantage of information she had learned from her husband.

Post-marital Agreements

These agreements can have an asset protection value if used correctly. Another couple, happily married for 30 years, used this tool to protect their personal assets. The husband's business was valued at $2,500,000 and their joint assets included a home, rental property, and cash worth about $2,500,000.

The husband's business was involved in a lawsuit, the outcome of which was unpredictable. The wife went to a family law attorney and drafted a post-marital separation agreement. In the agreement, the wife was to receive half of the couple's assets. She kept the home, rental property, and the cash, which was valued at $2,500,000, and the husband was to keep his business valued at $2,500,000.

Now the couple had no plan of separation and trusted each other completely. The agreement created a fair and equitable split of the couple's assets. Now if the husband lost his business lawsuit, the only thing he could lose was his business because his wife had sole entitlement to all the other assets.

Trusts

There are various ways to put assets in a trust that will protect them from most potential creditors. In this section I stress the importance of being a realistic optimist. **Plan for the worse and expect the best.** If you spend time structuring your financial affairs before trouble arises, you have the best chance of retaining your assets. You need to hire an estate lawyer. When you go to him, tell him everything.

Conclusion

New Beginnings

There are several kinds of people when it comes to business: people without knowledge, people with knowledge that don't use it to its full potential, and the winners. The winners are the people who have gained knowledge and continue to use it. Which one do you want to be? I hope the latter.

It's time to put what you have just begun to study into action. If you don't own the "Berman Differential Software Program" go to our website at www.BruceABerman.com and purchase it, you can't afford not to. With the tools available in my program, anyone with a desire to become a millionaire can take their newfound knowledge and apply it to the real world.

It's up to you. Ask yourself if you are ready to become a millionaire? You can't win the lottery if you don't buy a ticket. If you are a millionaire already, as many of my readers are, ask yourself if you want to substantially increase your net worth and protect your assets.

Set aside time each day and pick a section in this book, then apply it to your life. For example, take the "Analyzing a Potential Business Opportunity or Franchise" section. This section explains how there are countless potential business opportunities that you have been running into each day in daily living and before now never noticed. Now, armed with the knowledge and the tools of "The Berman Differential" program, you can recognize those opportunities and act on them. By brushing up on that chapter, it will assist you on a daily basis to look for ways to make more money without even going out of your way.

I have met thousands of business owners in my career and only a small amount of them know how to raise capital, and I can probably count on my fingers how many know how to take a company public. If you own a business or work for a business and want to expand that business, you need to start making a business plan now! "The Berman Differential Business Planning and Money Raising" Software CD works. How do I know it works? I know it works because I raised millions of dollars using that template and then took my own company public a few months later.

Today is the day for you to start down the road to your financial independence. Put "The Berman Differential" to work for you. Find or make that opportunity now. The only thing standing between you and making and keeping more money is fear. You have the tools–go use them.

My desire in creating "The Berman Differential" program was to assist as many people as possible in reaching their financial goals. I would love to hear how this program worked for you. Please feel free to send me an e-mail at CEO@BruceABerman.com.

Sincerely,

Bruce A. Berman

Bruce A. Berman

3-Day "Get Funded" Workshop

Our 3-day business development workshop/seminar will walk you through building your business plan, creating a slide-show presentation and presenting your business opportunity to investment bankers, all in one 3-day workshop!!!

We have proven our skills as business developers and communicators and in our three-day workshop we will polish your great ideas into investment ready written plans, create effective presentations then offer you a chance to present them to our network of investment sources before the end of the third day!

What happens the first day?

Our industry experts start by gathering knowledge of your product or service idea. From there, we can use our business plan and marketing know-how to facilitate and develop a clear, concise, and comprehensive business plan for you.

Second day is investor-show preparation.

Using our direct experience working with the investment community, we know what they are looking for, what their attention span is, and most importantly how to target and present the plan at any stage of a company's development. On the second day you will prepare and practice to present by acquiring:

"A Business Plan is your first impression. It gets you in the door and sets the tone. Use our proven methods because 'good enough' won't get you there."

- **A dynamite presentation for your plan,**
- **Training and practice sessions with our team.**
- **Proven closing techniques that can assist your company with a quick and favorable funding.**

Third day "Get funded"!

Finally, we carry your plan out to the end. The Berman Investment Group will place you in front of various investment bankers and assist you in presenting your plan. Remember, this is the part of the workshop where you could walk away with a check for your business.

To sign up for our 3-day "Get Funded" workshop
Call 877-5-BERMAN ext.17

The Berman Differential Software Collection

Now that you've learned the Money-Making lessons
I've used to make Millions of dollars for myself and
others, TAKE ACTION, use the software that can
help you make money in any business. The Berman
Differential software program, which consists of
4-business development software CDs, provides you
with the tools and resources you will need to take
your next steps towards wealth, financial success
and security!

The 4 money-making titles in the Berman Differential includes:

Business Plan and Money Raising Software

This CD was designed on the strength of 25 years experience developing and financing business plans. It utilizes the same plan format that Bruce A Berman employed to secure $4 million in funding and over $50,000,000 in equity in just 4 1/2 months! This useful tool allowed Mr. Berman to conceive of the ventures, develop a working plan, and present to investors in record time.

The Business planning CD is a Form based, Interactive CD that allows you to create, document and execute the type of planning that guides business from start-up to maturity. This easy-to-use software consists of a business plan template with 39 subject tabs that provide information about each topic within that subject.

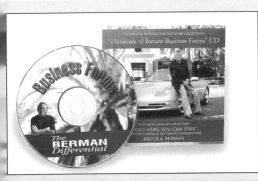

Hundreds of Instant Business Forms Software

In order to do business, you have to have the right documentation! Everything from purchase orders to Requests for Proposals. Many of the useful forms that help you to communicate in the language of business are made available to you through the Berman Differential's Hundreds of Business Forms CD. Bruce A Berman makes it perfectly clear, in his own words:

"My lawyer wanted $500 to draft a non disclosure agreement, which I knew was just a boilerplate form. This CD will save you hundreds of dollars, save you time and help you make money!"

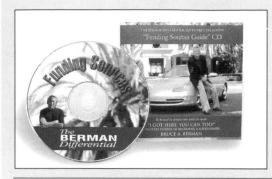

Funding Sources Software

In every business, cash flow is vital. Why use your own money to start and grow your business, when a variety of investors are searching for opportunities just like yours! The Funding Sources Directory is an information bank of over 1,500 companies that provide capital to businesses seeking financial support. Users will be able to view funding sources by keyword, state, or industry. Each funding source will have an information profile that will help the user to qualify them as a possible source of investment.

- **Minimum and maximum investment required**
- **The development stage in which sources seek to invest**
- **The company's address and contact information**
- **The type of investment source (private/public/Venture Capital)**
- **And a link to the funding company's website**

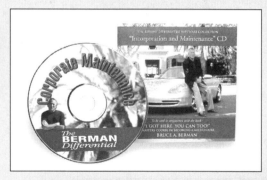

Incorporation and Corporate Maintenance Software

Becoming a corporation can be a confusing and expensive process. Understanding the benefits and protections afforded by incorporating can be the difference between success and failure in business. Knowing what type of corporation to become is crucial. The Berman Differential's Incorporation CD can help you get through the process cost effectively and time efficiently. If you are already incorporated, this software contains a collection of every corporate maintenance document required in each State.

inancial Success And ecurity is Just A Click Away!

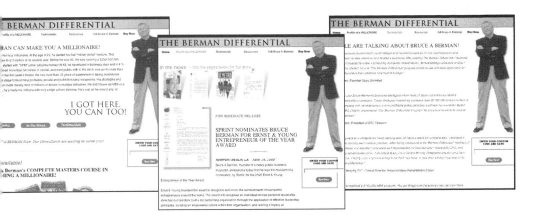

-OR-

all 877-5-BERMAN ext.17
Consultants are waiting to serve you!

Thank You,

Bruce A. Berman

Bruce A. Berman

Have A Profitable Business Day!

Notes